November 10–14, 2013
Pittsburgh, PA, USA

**Association for
Computing Machinery**

Advancing Computing as a Science & Profession

HILT'13

Proceedings of the ACM Conference on
High Integrity Language Technology

Sponsored by:
ACM SIGAda

In cooperation with:
ACM SIGAPP, ACM SIGBED, ACM SIGCAS, ACM SIGCSE, ACM SIGPLAN, ACM SIGSOFT, Ada-Europe, and Ada Resource Association

**Association for
Computing Machinery**

Advancing Computing as a Science & Profession

ISBN: 978-1-4503-2467-0

Welcome to ACM SIGAda's Annual International Conference High Integrity Language Technology – HILT 2013

Welcome to Pittsburgh and to HILT 2013, this year's annual international conference of the ACM Special Interest Group on the Ada Programming Language (SIGAda).

HILT 2013 features a top-quality technical program focused on the issues associated with **high integrity software** – where a failure could cause loss of human life or have other unacceptable consequences – and on the solutions provided by **language technology**. "Language technology" here encompasses not only programming languages but also languages for expressing specifications, program properties, domain models, and other attributes of the software or the overall system.

HILT 2013 consists of two days of tutorials, and three days of conference sessions. The **tutorials** cover a wide range of topics: Ada 2012, proving safety of parallel and multi-threaded programs, Formula 2.0: a language for formal specification and a tool for automated analysis, satisfiability modulo theories for high integrity development, practical specification and verification with code contracts, bounded model checking for high-integrity software, and service oriented architecture concepts and implementation.

The conference program includes **keynote and invited presentations** from internationally recognized experts:

- **Edmund M. Clarke** (Carnegie Mellon University, 2007 Turing Award Winner), on Model Checking and the Curse of Dimensionality;
- **Jeannette Wing** (Microsoft Research), on Formal Methods: An Industrial Perspective;
- **John Goodenough** (Carnegie Mellon University Software Engineering Institute), on Building Confidence in System Behavior; and
- **Michael Whalen** (University of Minnesota), on Up and Out: Scaling Formal Analysis Using Model-Based Development and Architecture Modeling.

HILT 2013 **conference sessions** deal with a range of topics associated with **safe, secure and reliable software**: formal verification technologies and toolsets, high-integrity parallel programing, model-based integration and code generation, architecture level design languages and compositional verification, and approaches to software safety and security. You will learn the latest developments in software verification technologies, and hear industrial presentations from practitioners. The accompanying **exhibits** will give you the opportunity to meet vendors and find out about their latest offerings. Vendors include AdaCore (Platinum Level); Microsoft Research (Gold Level); Ellidiss, Verocel (Silver Level); and LDRA, MathWorks (Basic Level).

At HILT 2013 you will learn about both the challenges confronting high integrity software and the solutions available to address them. Perhaps just as important are the social interactions that you get at a live conference: the chance to meet and talk with researchers and practitioners in industry, academia, and government, to ask them questions, and to explain your own work and interests. These renewed and new associations can be as valuable as the technical program at professional conferences, and their benefits will continue to reward you well after you return home.

HILT 2013 Conference Chair

Jeff Boleng
Carnegie Mellon University Software Engineering Institute

HILT 2013 Program Chair

S. Tucker Taft
AdaCore

Table of Contents

Model-Based Integration and Code Generation
Session Chair: Dirk Craeynest *(Consultant at Eurocontrol)*

Keynote Address – Building Confidence
Session Chair: Tucker Taft *(AdaCore)*

Architecture-Level Design Languages and Compositional Verification
Session Chair: Mike Feldman *(George Washington University (retired))*

Keynote Address – Formal Methods
Session Chair: Jeff L. Boleng *(Software Engineering Institute)*

Approaches to Software Safety and Security
Session Chair: Alok Srivastava *(TASC, Inc.)*

SIGAda HILT 2013 Conference Organization

Conference Chair:	Jeff Boleng *(The Software Engineering Institute)*
Program Chair:	S. Tucker Taft *(AdaCore)*
Exhibits and Sponsorships Chair:	Greg Gicca *(Verocel, Inc.)*
Proceedings Chair:	Jeff Boleng *(The Software Engineering Institute)*
Local Arrangements Chair:	Jeff Boleng *(The Software Engineering Institute)*
Workshops Chair:	John W. McCormick *(University of Northern Iowa)*
Publicity Chair:	Alok Srivastava *(TASC, Inc.)*
Treasurer:	Ricky E. Sward *(The MITRE Corporation)*
Registration Chair:	Michael Feldman *(George Washington Univ., retired)*
Tutorials Chair:	John W. McCormick *(University of Northern Iowa)*
Academic Community Liaison:	Michael Feldman *(George Washington Univ., retired)*
Webmaster:	Clyde Roby *(Institute for Defense Analyses)*
Logo Designer:	Weston Pan *(Raytheon Space and Airborne Systems)*
SIGAda Chair:	David Cook *(Stephen F. Austin State University)*
SIGAda Vice Chair for Meetings and Conferences:	S. Tucker Taft *(AdaCore)*
SIGAda International Representative:	Dirk Craeynest *(K. U. Leuven, Belgium)*
Program Committee:	S. Tucker Taft *(AdaCore)*
	Howard Ausden *(Lockheed Martin Corporation)*
	Ted Baker *(NSF and Florida State University)*
	Lennart Beringer *(Princeton University)*
	Judith Bishop *(Microsoft Research)*
	David Broman *(University of California, Berkeley)*
	Patrice Chalin *(Kansa State University)*
	Stephen Chong *(Harvard University)*
	Julien Delange *(Carnegie Mellon University, SEI)*
	Matthew Dwyer *(University of Nebraska, Lincoln)*
	Arjun Guha *(University of Massachusetts, Amherst)*
	David Hardin *(Rockwell Collins, Inc.)*
	Matt Heaney *(Google, Inc.)*
	James Hunt *(aicas, Germany)*

**Program Committee
(continued)**

Luke Hutchison *(Google, Inc.)*

Y. Annie Liu *(SUNY at Stony Brook)*

Francesco Logozzo *(Microsoft Research)*

Niko Matsakis *(Mozilla Research)*

Yannick Moy *(AdaCore)*

David Pearce *(Victoria University of Wellington, New Zealand)*

Michael Norrish *(NICTA, Australia)*

Erhard Ploedereder *(University of Stuttgart, Germany)*

Jean-Pierre Rosen *(Adalog, France)*

Sukyoung Ryu *(KAIST -- Korean Advanced Institute of Science and Technology, Korea)*

Julien Signoles *(French Alternative Energies and Atomic Energy Commission, France)*

Konrad Slind *(Rockwell Collins, Inc.)*

Joyce Tokar *(Pyrrhus Software)*

Eric Van Wyk *(University of Minnesota)*

Jack Wileden *(University of Massachusetts, Amherst)*

HILT 2013 Sponsors

Sponsor:

In cooperation with:

Tutorial: Proving Safety of Parallel / Multi-Threaded Programs

S. Tucker Taft

AdaCore

24 Muzzey Street, 3rd Floor

Lexington, MA 02421 USA

+1-781-750-8068 x220

taft@adacore.com

ABSTRACT

This tutorial will introduce the attendees to analysis and proof techniques for programs using parallelism and multi-threading. There are no specific prerequisites, but a familiarity with the notions of preconditions and postconditions, aliasing, race conditions, and deadlocks would be of value. The examples will be based on the threading and parallelism models of *Java*, *Ada*, and two new parallel languages, one called *ParaSail* [4] and another, inspired by the verifiable SPARK[1][2] subset of Ada, called *Sparkel*[3]. We will introduce the distinction between safety and liveness properties, and then focus primarily on techniques for the verification of safety properties, including the absence of race conditions and deadlocks. We will also discuss the issue of determinism vs. non-determinism in parallel and multi-threaded programs.

Categories and Subject Descriptors

D.1.3 [**Programming Techniques**]: Concurrent Programming – parallel programming; D.2.4 [Software Engineering]: Software/Program Verification – formal methods, reliability; [**Programming Languages**]: Language Constructs and Features – concurrent programming structures.

General Terms

Algorithms, Languages, Verification.

Keywords

Parallel programming, multithreading, Java, Ada, SPARK, ParaSail, race condition detection, deadlock detection.

1. INTRODUCTION

This tutorial will introduce the attendees to analysis and proof techniques for programs using parallelism and multi-threading. There are no specific prerequisites, but a familiarity with the notions of preconditions and postconditions, aliasing, race conditions, and deadlocks would be of value. The examples will be based on the threading and parallelism models of *Java*, *Ada*, and two new parallel languages, one called *ParaSail*[4] and another, inspired by the verifiable SPARK[1][2] subset of Ada, called *Sparkel*[3]. We will introduce the distinction between safety and liveness properties, and then focus primarily on techniques for the verification of safety properties, including the absence of race conditions and deadlocks. We will also discuss

HILT'13, November 10–14, 2013, Pittsburgh, PA, USA.

ACM 978-1-4503-2467-0/13/11.

http://dx.doi.org/10.1145/2527269.2527279

the issue of determinism vs. non-determinism in parallel and multi-threaded programs.

2. OUTLINE

The overall outline for the tutorial is as follows:

1) Introduction to formal verification of parallel and multi-threaded programs

    a) Is there an agreed-upon distinction between parallelism and multi-threading?

    b) What are the goals of formal verification vs. verification by testing?

    c) What are the fundamental verification issues for concurrent programming relative to sequential programming?

    d) How does non-determinism affect verification of concurrent systems?

    e) What tools and technologies are available for verification of concurrent systems?

2) Safety properties vs. Liveness properties

    a) Examples of safety vs. liveness properties in concurrent systems.

    b) Relation to safety, correctness, and termination concerns in sequential systems.

    c) Overall approaches to safety verification vs. liveness verification.

3) Unsafe race conditions

    a) How can we define a race condition, what makes a race condition safe or unsafe, in both lock-based and lock-free data structures?

    b) How can unsafe race conditions be detected statically, and are there modular approaches to race condition detection?

    c) How do race conditions relate to non-determinism?

    d) Are there language features which can help to minimize the possibility of race conditions?

4) Deadlock detection and prevention

    a) How is "deadlock" defined, and what distinguishes a "deadlock" from a "livelock"?

    b) What are the typical causes of deadlock, and how are deadlocks detected dynamically?

c) How is the possibility of deadlock detected statically, and are there modular analysis approaches?

d) Are there language features which can help in the static prevention of deadlocks?

5) Liveness and other safety properties

a) Proof of "progress" in concurrent systems, including in the presence of lock-free data structures.

b) Definitions of "fairness" and relation to real-time scheduling issues.

c) Predicting real-time performance and resource utilization in parallel systems.

6) Summary and Conclusions

3. REFERENCES

[1] Chapman, R., *Industrial experience with SPARK*, Ada Letters. XX(4), 64–68 (2000).

[2] SPARK Team, *SPARK Examiner, The SPARK Ravenscar Profile*, Praxis, 2008, available at: http://intelligent-systems.altran.com/fileadmin/medias/0.commons/documents/Technology_documents/examiner_ravenscar.pdf (retrieved 8/2013)..

[3] *Sparkel* web site, http://www.sparkel.org .

[4] Taft, S. Tucker, *ParaSail: Less is More with Multicore*, www.embedded.com, 2012, available at http://www.embedded.com/design/other/4375616/ParaSail--Less-is-more-with-multicore (retrieved 9/23/2013).

Engineering Domain-Specific Languages with FORMULA 2.0

[Tutorial]

Ethan K. Jackson
Microsoft Research
One Microsoft Way
Redmond, WA 98052
ejackson@microsoft.com

ABSTRACT

Domain-specific languages (DSLs) are useful for capturing and reusing engineering expertise. They can formalize industrial patterns and practices while increasing the scalability of verification, because input programs are written at a higher level of abstraction. However, engineering new DSLs with custom verification is a non-trivial task in its own right, and usually requires programming language, formal methods, and automated theorem proving expertise.

In this tutorial we present FORMULA 2.0, which is formal framework for developing DSLs. FORMULA specifications are succinct descriptions of DSLs, and specifications can be immediately connected to state-of-the-art analysis engines without additional expertise. FORMULA provides: (1) succinct specifications of DSLs and compilers, (2) efficient compilation and execution of input programs, (3) program synthesis and compiler verification.

We take a unique approach to provide these features: Specifications are written as *strongly-typed* [3, 6] *open-world logic programs* [4]. These specifications are highly declarative and easily express rich synthesis / verification problems. Automated reasoning is enabled by efficient symbolic execution of logic programs into quantifier-free sub-problems, which are dispatched to the state-of-the-art SMT solver Z3 [1]. FORMULA has been applied within Microsoft to develop DSLs for verifiable device drivers and protocols [2]. It has been used by the automotive / embedded systems industries for software / hardware co-design [5] and design-space exploration [7] under hard resource allocation constraints. It is being used to develop semantic specifications for complex cyber-physical systems [8].

Categories and Subject Descriptors

D.2.2 [**Software Engineering**]: Design Tools and Techniques

Permission to make digital or hard copies of part or all of this work for personal or classroom use is granted without fee provided that copies are not made or distributed for profit or commercial advantage, and that copies bear this notice and the full citation on the first page. Copyrights for third-party components of this work must be honored. For all other uses, contact the owner/author(s). Copyright is held by the author/owner(s).
HILT'13, November 12–14, 2013, Pittsburgh, PA, USA.
ACM 978-1-4503-2467-0/13/11.
http://dx.doi.org/10.1145/2527269.2527286 .

General Terms

Design

Keywords

Domain-specific languages, formal specifications

1. DOMAINS

The static semantics of DSLs are specified using algebraic data types and open-world logic programs (OLPs). *Domain modules* hold these definitions.

Example 1 (Deployment DSL).

```
1: domain Deployments
2: {
3:    Service  ::= new (name: String).
4:    Node     ::= new (id: Natural).
5:    Conflict ::= new (s1: Service, s2: Service).
6:    Deploy   ::= fun (s: Service => n: Node).
7:
8:    conforms no { n | Deploy(s, n), Deploy(s', n),
9:                      Conflict(s, s') }.
10: }
```

The *Deployments* domain formalizes the following deployment problem: There are services, which can be in conflict, and nodes, which can run services. Services must be deployed to nodes such that no node executes conflicting services. Lines 3 - 6 introduce data types for the entities of the DSL. The *conformance rule* (lines 8 - 9) forbids conflicting tasks to run on the same node. Constructing a conforming "program" for a fixed set of tasks, conflicts, and nodes is NP-complete. It is equivalent to coloring the conflict graph with nodes.

2. MODELS

"Programs" are a represented as sets of well-typed ground facts w.r.t. some domain. *Model modules* hold these ground facts.

Example 2 (Several deployments).

```
1: model Undeployed of Deployments
2: {
3:    sVoice is Service("Voice Recognition").
4:    sDB   is Service("Big Database").
```

```
5:    n0      is Node(0).
6:    n1      is Node(1).
7:    Conflict(sVoice, sDB).
8: }
9: model Good of Deployments extends Undeployed
10: {
11:    Deploy(sVoice, n0).
12:    Deploy(sDB, n1).
13: }
14: model Bad of Deployments extends Undeployed
15: {
16:    Deploy(sVoice, n0).
17:    Deploy(sDB, n0).
18: }
```

Formally, a domain D is an OLP. A model M *closes* D with a set of facts, written $D[M]$. The properties of a model M are those properties provable by the closed logic program $D[M]$. For example:

- $Deployments[Undeployed] \not\models conforms$, because services are not deployed to nodes.

- $Deployments[Good] \models conforms$, because all services are deployed and all conflicts are respected.

- $Deployments[Bad] \not\models conforms$, because its deployments violate conflicts.

3. PARTIAL MODELS

Partial models partially close domains. A partial model P is *solved* by a model M if all assertions and *requires clauses* of P hold in $D[M]$. In this way, partial models describe problem instances. The partial model below describes a specific deployment problem.

Example 3 (A deployment problem).

```
1: partial model SpecificProblem of Deployments
2: {
3:    requires Deployments.conforms.
4:
5:    sVoice is Service("Voice Recognition").
6:    sDB    is Service("Big Database").
7:    n0     is Node(0).
8:    n1     is Node(1).
9:    Conflict(sVoice, sDB).
10: }
```

The assertions in lines 5 - 9 must hold in a solution. Requires clauses state more complex requirements on solutions, e.g. line 3 requires models to conform to the Deployments domain. The *Good* model is a solution (Example 2, lines 9 - 13).

4. TRANSFORMS

Transforms are OLPs that transform models between domains. They are useful for formalizing operational semantics, compilers, and product constructions.

Example 4 (A compiler).

```
1: transform Compile (in::Deployments)
2: returns (out::NodeConfigs)
3: {
```

```
4:    out.Config(n.id, list) :-
5:       n is in.Node,
6:       list = toList(out.#Services, NIL,
7:                     { s.name | in.Deploy(s, n) }).
8: }
9: domain NodeConfigs
10: {
11:    Config ::=
12:       fun (loc: Natural ->
13:            list: any Services + { NIL }).
14:    Services ::=
15:       new (name: String,
16:            tail: any Services + { NIL }).
17: }
```

Models of the *NodeConfigs* domain contain node configuration files (lines 9 - 17). Each file lists the services that run on a node. These are modeled using recursive ADTs. The *Compile* transform takes a *Deployments* model called *in* and produces a *NodeConfigs* model called *out*. This is accomplished by the *rule* in lines 4 - 7. This rule converts every node into a configuration file containing a list of services.

5. CONCLUSION

We have demonstrated a few of the key concepts provided by FORMULA 2.0 for defining and reasoning about DSLs. Additionally, domains, models, and transforms can be composed to build complex specifications. Transforms can be verified using the same model finding techniques for solving partial models. Rules can contain rich constraints, such as arithmetic, string, and list constraints. More information can be found at http://research.microsoft.com/formula.

6. REFERENCES

[1] L. M. de Moura and N. Bjørner. Satisfiability modulo theories: introduction and applications. *Commun. ACM*, 54(9):69–77, 2011.

[2] A. Desai, V. Gupta, E. K. Jackson, S. Qadeer, S. K. Rajamani, and D. Zufferey. P: safe asynchronous event-driven programming. In *PLDI*, pages 321–332, 2013.

[3] E. K. Jackson, N. Bjørner, and W. Schulte. Canonical regular types. In *ICLP (Technical Communications)*, pages 73–83, 2011.

[4] E. K. Jackson, N. Bjørner, and W. Schulte. Open-world logic programs: A new foundation for formal specifications. Technical Report MSR-TR-2013-55, Microsoft Research, 2013. http://research.microsoft.com/pubs/192963/MSR-TR-2013-55.pdf.

[5] E. K. Jackson, E. Kang, M. Dahlweid, D. Seifert, and T. Santen. Components, Platforms and Possibilities: Towards Generic Automation for MDA. In *EMSOFT*, pages 39–48, 2010.

[6] E. K. Jackson, W. Schulte, and N. Bjørner. Detecting specification errors in declarative languages with constraints. In *MoDELS*, pages 399–414, 2012.

[7] E. K. Jackson, G. Simko, and J. Sztipanovits. Diversely Enumerating System-Level Architectrues. In *EMSOFT*, 2013.

[8] G. Simko, D. Lindecker, T. Levendovszky, S. Neema, and J. Sztipanovits. Formal semantics specification of cyber-physical components integration and composition. In *MoDELS*, 2013.

Satisfiability Modulo Theories for High Integrity Development

Nikolaj Bjørner
Microsoft Research

Satisfiability Modulo Theories (SMT) solvers are used in many modern program verification, analysis and testing tools. They owe their scale and efficiency thanks to advances in search algorithms underlying modern satisfiability solvers for propositional logic (SAT solvers) and first-order theorem provers, and they owe their versatility in software development applications thanks to specialized algorithms supporting theories, such as numbers and algebraic data-types, of relevance for software engineering. This tutorial introduces SMT solvers in the context of development of high integrity software. We introduce the algorithmic principles of SMT solving, including the foundations of modern SAT solving search, integration with specialized theory solvers, and modules for quantifier reasoning. The second part of the tutorial shows how the capabilities of SMT solvers can be used in applications where a high degree of integrity is sought. To illustrate various uses of SMT solving we take as starting point some of the tools using the state-of-the-art SMT solver Z3 from Microsoft Research.

The introduction to the algorithms behind SMT solvers is aimed to give an idea of the capabilities of modern SMT solvers: what problems are a good fit for SMT solvers and what areas are challenging or out of scope. The applications examined in the second part of the tutorial include Pex (a tool based on symbolic execution), SecGuru (a tool used for firewall analysis), Dafny (a program verification environment), and FORMULA (a tool used for model based design). The tutorial use these examples to illustrate how SMT solvers are integrated within analysis tools and how to leverage the SMT solvers when using such tools.

Familiarity with basic concepts from programming languages and logic will be assumed. On the other hand the tutorial does not assume familiarity with how SMT solvers work or how to use them.

Z3 is developed by Leonardo de Moura, Nikolaj Bjorner and Christoph Wintersteiger. There are online demos and tutorials available from `http://rise4fun.com/z3` (a text-based interface using the SMT-LIB2 language). Several tools shown on `http://rise4fun.com` use Z3 under the hood. Z3 binaries and the source code can be downloaded from `http://z3.codeplex.com`.

Categories and Subject Descriptors

F.3.1 [**LOGICS AND MEANINGS OF PROGRAMS**]: Specifying and Verifying and Reasoning about Programs; F.3.2 [**MATHEMATICAL LOGIC AND FORMAL LANGUAGES**]: Mathematical Logic

Keywords

SMT, SAT, Theorem Proving, Program Verification, Testing, Model based design

HILT'13, November 12–14, 2013, Pittsburgh, PA, USA.
ACM 978-1-4503-2467-0/13/11.

Practical Specification and Verification with CodeContracts

Francesco Logozzo
Microsoft Research
One Microsoft Way, Redmond, WA, USA
logozzo@microsoft.com

ABSTRACT

In this tutorial I will introduce CodeContracts, the .NET solution for contract specifications. CodeContracts consist of a language and compiler-agnostic API to express contracts, and of a set of tools to automatically generate the documentation and to perform dynamic and static verification. The CodeContracts API is part of .NET since v4, the tools are available for download on the Visual Studio Gallery. To date, they have been downloaded more than 100,000 times.

Categories and Subject Descriptors

D [**Software**]: Miscellaneous; D.2.1 [**Software Engineering**]: Requirements/Specifications; D.2.4 [**Software Engineering**]: Software/Program Verification—*Assertion checkers,Programming by contract*

General Terms

Contracts,Verification

Keywords

Abstract Interpretation,Contracts,Inference,Program Verification

1. INTRODUCTION

Contracts are a popular software design methodology [15]. They are based on the idea that software modules should expose a well-defined interface, clearly stating the properties each module expects on the input and ensures on the output values. In object-oriented languages, contracts take the form of an invariant attached to the object and of preconditions and postconditions attached to the methods.

Traditionally a programmer who wants to use contracts has two choices. The first one is to adopt a programming language which has first class support for contracts, as for instance Eiffel [15] or Spark [1]. The second one is to keep the language she is used to, but to use a different compiler

HILT 2013 Nov 10-14 2013, Pittsburgh, PA, USA
ACM ACM 978-1-4503-2466-3/13/11
http://dx.doi.org/10.1145/2527269.2527282 .

opportunely extended to support contracts, *e.g.*, JML [12] or Spec# [2] respectively extending Java and C#. The advantages of the first choice are the evident beauty and uniformity provided by having language support for contracts. The main disadvantages is the requirement to learn a new programming language and new libraries. The second choice mitigates those problems, but it has the (big) practical the drawback of asking the programmer to trust a non-standard compiler.

CodeContracts [3] provide a third option, which overcomes the problems above by using a library-based approach. With a library, there is no need to adopt a new language or a new compiler. Writing contracts is as difficult as invoking as function.

2. CODECONTRACTS

The main insight of CodeContracts is that code can be specified with code. We have developed a contract library and a set of tools that consume those contracts. CodeContracts originated from the Spec# project, where the language-based approach to contracts was replaced with a library-based one and the deductive verification-based static analysis tool was replaced by an abstract interpretation-based one.

2.1 API

Since .NET v4, the static class `System.Diagnostic.Contracts.Contract` contains the definitions for CodeContracts. The class contains methods to express preconditions, postconditions, object invariants, assertions, assumptions, and legacy requires. It also defines: (i) a few helper methods used as placeholder for the method return value and the old value of some element of the prestate; (ii) the attributes to help the tools find the contracts for abstract methods and interfaces. All members of the `Contract` class are conditionally defined.

2.2 Dynamic verification

We have developed `ccrewrite`, a tool to perform the runtime checking of contracts. The tool runs as a post-build step. It performs rewriting of the binary. It takes care of basic things as inheriting contracts and inserting postconditions and object invariants checkings at the right spots. But it has also some more advanced options, to provide: (i) customizable behavior for contract violation — *e.g.*, throw an exception, behave as an assertion violation, user-defined ...; (ii) fine-grain tuning of the contract checking — *e.g.*, check preconditions at call site, skip quantifier checks, check only public surface contracts ....

2.3 Static verification

Unlike most of existing solutions, we use abstract interpretation [5] for static verification. Abstract interpretation: (i) provides a high level of automation —*e.g.*, no need to specify loop invariants, which are automatically inferred; (ii) enables a fine tuning of the analyzer towards the properties to prove; (iii) guarantees scalability. Our static verification tool, `cccheck` [9], analyzes each method in isolation, infers the properties of interest [11, 10, 14, 7], and it uses those properties to prove user-provided contracts (*e.g.*, preconditions, postconditions) and language-induced contracts(*e.g.*, absence of null-pointers, buffer overruns). When it fails to prove a contract, it suggest a verified code repair [13]. It infers preconditions [6], postconditions, and object invariants [4] which are propagated to the callers. It uses a database to cache the analysis results, ensuring scalability and sharing of results among team members. It uses advanced heuristics to prioritize warnings and to eliminate false positives.

2.4 Other tools

We have developed tools to automatically generate the documentation from CodeContracts and to enhance Visual Studio to show contracts while typing. Furthermore, we integrated all our tools in Visual Studio [8], so that: (i) they can be configured from within it; (ii) the errors and the alarms are presented in the programmer's usual environment.

2.5 Adoption

CodeContracts are increasingly adopted inside and outside Microsoft. They are available for download from the Visual Studio Gallery [16]. We frequently interact with our external customers via an external forum. The interaction with the customers enables us to improve the quality of the tools, fix bugs, add new features, and answer common and tricky questions on contracts.

3. REFERENCES

[1] J. Barnes. *High Integrity Software: The SPARK Approach to Safety and Security*. Addison-Wesley, 2003.

[2] M. Barnett, M. Fähndrich, K. R. M. Leino, P. Müller, W. Schulte, and H. Venter. Specification and verification: the Spec# experience. *Commun. ACM*, 54(6):81–91, 2011.

[3] M. Barnett, M. Fähndrich, and F. Logozzo. Embedded contract languages. In *SAC'10*. ACM Press, 2010.

[4] M. Bouaziz, L. Logozzo, and M. Fähndrich. Inference of necessary field conditions with abstract interpretation. In *APLAS*, 2012.

[5] P. Cousot and R. Cousot. Abstract interpretation: a unified lattice model for static analysis of programs by construction or approximation of fixpoints. In *POPL'77*. ACM Press, Jan. 1977.

[6] P. Cousot, R. Cousot, M. Fähndrich, and F. Logozzo. Automatic inference of necessary preconditions. In *VMCAI*, pages 128–148, 2013.

[7] P. Cousot, R. Cousot, and F. Logozzo. A parametric segmentation functor for fully automatic and scalable array content analysis. In *POPL 2011*. ACM Press, Jan. 2011.

[8] M. Fahndrich, M. Barnett, D. Leijen, and F. Logozzo. Integrating a set of contract checking tools into visual studio. In *TOPI*. IEEE, 2012.

[9] M. Fähndrich and F. Logozzo. Static contract checking with abstract interpretation. In *FoVeOOS*, 2010.

[10] P. Ferrara, F. Logozzo, and M. Fähndrich. Safer unsafe code in .NET. In *OOPSLA'08*. ACM Press, 2008.

[11] V. Laviron and F. Logozzo. Subpolyhedra: A (more) scalable approach to infer linear inequalities. In *VMCAI '09*, 2009.

[12] G. T. Leavens, J. R. Kiniry, and E. Poll. A jml tutorial: Modular specification and verification of functional behavior for java. In *CAV*, 2007.

[13] F. Logozzo and T. Ball. Modular and verified automatic program repair. In *OOPSLA*. ACM, 2012.

[14] F. Logozzo and M. Fähndrich. Pentagons: a weakly relational abstract domain for the efficient validation of array accesses. In *SAC*. ACM, 2008.

[15] B. Meyer. *Eiffel: The Language*. Prentice Hall, 1991.

[16] Microsoft. Codecontracts tools. http://aka.ms/codecontracts/vsgallery.

HILT'13 Tutorial Overview / Bounded Model Checking of High-Integrity Software

Sagar Chaki
Carnegie Mellon Software Engineering Institute
4500 Fifth Avenue
Pittsburgh, PA 15213, USA
chaki@sei.cmu.edu

1. ABSTRACT

Model checking [5] is an automated algorithmic technique for exhaustive verification of systems, described as finite state machines, against temporal logic [9] specifications. It has been used successfully to verify hardware at an industrial scale [6]. One of the most successful variants of model checking is Bounded Model Checking (BMC) [2] which leverages the power of state-of-the-art satisfiability (SAT) [1] and satisfiability-modulo-theory (SMT) [2] to push the boundaries of automated verification. Like model checking, BMC was developed originally for hardware, but has since been extended and applied successfully to verify sequential [4], multi-threaded [1, 10], as well as real-time software [3].

A key benefit of BMC-based software model checkers, such as CBMC [4], is that they are able to handle bit-level semantics of programs precisely. Thus, they are able to detect errors due to integer overflows, and prove correctness of programs that use bit-level operations, without reporting false warnings, or missing bugs. This makes BMC ideal for verifying high-integrity software, where the cost of failure is substantial. Indeed, CBMC has been used to verify a wide variety of low-level safety and security-critical systems, such as co-pilots [8], OS schedulers [7], and hypervisors [11] (see http://www.cprover.org/cbmc/applications.shtml for a more expansive list).

This tutorial will provide an introduction to BMC, its underlying technical principles, and applications to verifying sequential, multi-threaded, and real-time software. The tutorial will be hands-on, with live demonstrations of using BMC tools for verifying sample programs written in C.

Categories and Subject Descriptors

D.2.4 [**Software/Program Verification**]: Model checking; F.3.1 [**Specifying and Verifying and Reasoning about Programs**]: Mechanical verification

---

[1] http://www.satcompetition.org

[2] http://www.smtlib.org

HILT'13, November 10–14, 2013, Pittsburgh, PA, USA.
ACM 978-1-4503-2467-0/13/11.
http://dx.doi.org/10.1145/2527269.2527288.

Keywords

Model Checking; Verification; Bounded Model Checking; Software Verification; Real-Time Software

2. OUTLINE

The total duration of the tutorial is 3.5 hours. The topics to be covered (including estimated duration of each topic) are:

1. Overview of model checking (15 mins)

2. Overview of SAT/SMT solving (15 mins)

3. Bounded model checking of hardware – connecting model checking and SMT (20 mins)

4. Bounded model checking of single-threaded C code (50 mins)

   - Technical details (verification condition generation etc.)
   - Hands-on demonstration using the CBMC [4] tool
     - http://www.cprover.org/cbmc

5. Bounded model checking of multi-threaded C code (30 mins)

   - Technical details (sequentialization for multi-threaded code)
   - Hands-on demonstration using the CBMC tool

6. Bounded model checking of periodic real-time software (50 mins)

   - Technical details (sequentialization for periodic programs)
   - Hands-on demonstration using the REKH [3] tool
     - http://www.andrew.cmu.edu/~arieg/Rek

7. Summary, Ongoing and Future Work, Q&A (30 mins)

3. INTENDED AUDIENCE

This tutorial is aimed primarily at someone looking for a hands on introduction to bounded model checking for single-threaded, multi-threaded, and periodic real-time software, e.g., someone with a background in software development, compilers, static analysis, software quality, programming languages etc. Knowledge about one or more of the following topics is desirable:

1. Compiler internals (e.g., control flow graphs, static single assignment).

2. Propositional logic and satisfiability.

3. Familiarity with an imperative programming language (C preferred).

4. No prior knowledge about model checking, temporal logic etc. needed.

4. PRESENTER INFORMATION

Sagar Chaki is a senior Member of Technical Staff at the Software Engineering Institute at Carnegie Mellon University. He received a B.Tech in Computer Science & Engineering from the Indian Institute of Technology, Kharagpur in 1999, and a Ph.D. in Computer Science from Carnegie Mellon University in 2005. These days, he works mainly on model checking software for real-time and cyber-physical systems, but he is generally interested in rigorous and automated approaches for improving software quality. He has developed several automated software verification tools, including two model checkers for C programs, MAGIC [3] and Copper [4]. He has co-authored over 50 peer reviewed publications. More details about Sagar and his current work can be found at http://www.contrib.andrew.cmu.edu/~schaki.

5. ACKNOWLEDGMENT

Copyright 2013 ACM. This material is based upon work funded and supported by the Department of Defense under Contract No. FA8721-05-C-0003 with Carnegie Mellon University for the operation of the Software Engineering Institute, a federally funded research and development center.

6. REFERENCES

[1] J. Alglave, D. Kroening, V. Nimal, and M. Tautschnig. Software Verification for Weak Memory via Program Transformation. In M. Felleisen and P. Gardner, editors, *Proceedings of the 22nd European Symposium On Programming (ESOP '13)*, volume 7792 of *Lecture Notes in Computer Science*, pages 512–532, Rome, Italy, March 2013. Springer-Verlag.

[2] A. Biere, A. Cimatti, E. M. Clarke, O. Strichman, and Y. Zue. *Bounded Model Checking*, volume 58 of *Advances in computers*. Academic Press, 2003.

[3] S. Chaki, A. Gurfinkel, S. Kong, and O. Strichman. Compositional Sequentialization of Periodic Programs. In R. Giacobazzi, J. Berdine, and I. Mastroeni, editors, *Proceedings of the 14th International Conference on Verification, Model Checking, and Abstract Interpretation (VMCAI '13)*, volume 7737 of *Lecture Notes in Computer Science*, pages 536–554, Rome, Italy. New York, January 2013. Springer-Verlag.

[4] E. Clarke, D. Kroening, and F. Lerda. A Tool for Checking ANSI-C Programs. In K. Jensen and A. Podelski, editors, *Proceedings of the 10th International Conference on Tools and Algorithms for the Construction and Analysis of Systems (TACAS '04)*, volume 2988 of *Lecture Notes in Computer Science*, pages 168–176, Barcelona, Spain, March 29–April 2, 2004. New York, NY, March–April 2004. Springer-Verlag.

[5] E. M. Clarke, E. A. Emerson, and J. Sifakis. Model checking: algorithmic verification and debugging. *Communications of the ACM (CACM)*, 52(11):74–84, November 2009.

[6] E. M. Clarke, O. Grumberg, H. Hiraishi, S. Jha, D. E. Long, K. L. McMillan, and L. A. Ness. Verification of the Futurebus+ Cache Coherence Protocol. *Formal Methods in System Design (FMSD)*, 6(2):217–232, March 1995.

[7] M. K. Ludwich and A. A. Fröhlich. On the formal verification of component-based embedded operating systems. *Operating Systems Review*, 46(1):28–34, 2013.

[8] L. Pike, S. Niller, and N. Wegmann. Runtime Verification for Ultra-Critical Systems. In S. Khurshid and K. Sen, editors, *Proceedings of the 2nd International Conference on Runtime Verification (RV '11)*, volume 7186 of *Lecture Notes in Computer Science*, pages 310–324, San Francisco, CA, USA, September 2011. Springer-Verlag.

[9] A. Pnueli. The Temporal Logic of Programs. In *Proceedings of the 18th Annual Symposium on Foundations of Computer Science (FOCS '77)*, pages 46–57, Providence, RI, October 31–November 2, 1977. New York, NY, October–November 1977. IEEE Computer Society.

[10] N. Sinha and C. Wang. Staged concurrent program analysis. In *Proceedings of the 18th ACM SIGSOFT Symposium on Foundations of Software Engineering (FSE '10)*, pages 47–56, Santa Fe, NM, USA, November 7-11, 2010, November 2010. Association for Computing Machinery.

[11] A. Vasudevan, S. Chaki, L. Jia, J. M. McCune, J. Newsome, and A. Datta. Design, Implementation and Verification of an eXtensible and Modular Hypervisor Framework. In *Proceedings of the 34th IEEE Symposium on Security and Privacy (Oakland '13)*, pages 430–444, San Francisco, CA, USA, May 2013. IEEE Computer Society.

---

[3] http://www.cs.cmu.edu/~chaki/magic/
[4] http://www.sei.cmu.edu/predictability/tools/copper/

Service-Oriented Architecture (SOA) Concepts and Implementations

Ricky E. Sward
The MITRE Corporation
1155 Academy Park Loop
Colorado Springs, CO 80910
rsward@mitre.org

Jeff Boleng
The Software Engineering Institute
Carnegie Mellon University
4500 Fifth Avenue
Pittsburgh, PA 15213
jlboleng@sei.cmu.edu

ABSTRACT

This tutorial explains how to implement a Service-Oriented Architecture (SOA) for reliable systems using an Enterprise Service Bus (ESB) and the Ada Web Server (AWS). The first part of the tutorial describes terms of Service-Oriented Architectures (SOA) including service, service registry, service provider, service consumer, Service Oriented Architecture Protocol (SOAP), and Web Service Description Language (WSDL). This tutorial also presents principles of SOA including loose coupling, encapsulation, composability of web services, and statelessness of web services. The tutorial also covers the benefits of SOA and organizations that are supporting SOA infrastructure. The second part of the tutorial covers the Enterprise Service Bus (ESB) including definitions, capabilities, benefits and drawbacks. The tutorial discusses the difference between SOA and an ESB, as well as some of the commercially available ESB solutions on the market. The Mule ESB is explored in more detail and several examples are given. In the third part, the tutorial covers the Ada Web Server (AWS) built using the Ada programming language. The tutorial covers the capabilities of AWS and explains how to build and install AWS. The tutorial explains how to build an AWS server and include the server in an Ada application. The tutorial demonstrates how to build a call back function in AWS and build a response to a SOAP message. Finally, the tutorial explains how to connect an AWS server to an ESB endpoint. AWS is a key component to building a SOA for a reliable system. This capability allows the developer to expose services in a high-integrity system using the Ada and SPARK programming languages.

Categories and Subject Descriptors

D.2.11 Software, SOFTWARE ENGINEERING, Software Architectures

Keywords

Ada, Service Oriented Architectures

HILT'13, November 10–14, 2013, Pittsburgh, PA, USA.
ACM 978-1-4503-2467-0/13/11.
http://dx.doi.org/10.1145/2527269.2527289

1. DETAILED OUTLINE

1. Introduction and Background
2. Part 1 – Service-Oriented Architecture
   a. SOA Background Terminology: XML, XML Document, XSD, XSLT
   b. SOA Terminology: Service, Registry, Provider, Consumer, WSDL, SOAP, SLA
   c. SOA Message Patterns: Request/Response, Publish/Subscribe
   d. SOA Orchestration and Web Service Security
   e. Principles of SOA
   f. Benefits of SOA
   g. SOA Organizations: W3C, OASIS
3. Part 2 – Enterprise Service Bus (ESB)
   a. ESB description and terminology
   b. Commercial ESB options
   c. ESB's and SOA
   d. Mule ESB Case Study and examples
      i. Mule endpoints
      ii. Mule configuration file
4. Part 3 – Ada Web Server (AWS)
   a. AWS definitions and capabilities
   b. Building and Installing AWS
   c. Building an AWS web server
   d. Building a call-back function
   e. AWS server example
   f. AWS and WSDLs
5. Connecting AWS to Mule
   a. Configuration file
   b. Building an Ada web service
   c. Exposing an Ada web service
   d. Example
6. Conclusions

2. ABOUT THE PRESENTERS

Ricky E. "Ranger" Sward is a Lead Information Systems Engineer for the MITRE Corporation in Colorado Springs, CO, USA. He currently supports a project to develop data and video collaboration widgets for the Army's DCGS-A system. He is also supporting an internal MITRE research project on 3D printed Unmanned Aircraft Systems and Android control of robots. Ranger retired from the US Air Force in August 2006 after a 21 year career as a Communications and Computer officer. He taught at the US Air Force Academy for 10 years where he taught courses such as Software Engineering and Unmanned Aircraft Systems. He has a B.S. and an M.S. in Computer Science, as well as a Ph.D. in Computer Engineering. He is currently the Past Chair of ACM SIGAda.

Jeff Boleng is a research scientist in the Advanced Mobile Systems group at the Software Engineering Institute, Carnegie Mellon University, in Pittsburgh, PA, USA. His current research focus is enabling rich computing applications and data at the tactical edge. He is also researching techniques for widespread software portability and attack surface characterization of mobile devices. His past operational Air Force Experience includes evaluating and implementing SOA solutions for command and control and knowledge management applications. He is a 1991 graduate of the US Air Force Academy and has an M.S. and Ph.D. in Mathematical and Computer Sciences from Colorado School of Mines.

Technology for Inferring Contracts from Code

Francesco Logozzo
Microsoft Research
One Microsoft Way, Redmond, WA, USA
logozzo@microsoft.com

ABSTRACT

Contracts are a simple yet very powerful form of specification. They consists of method preconditions and post-conditions, of object invariants, and of assertions and loop invariants. Ideally, the programmer will annotate all of her code with contracts which are mechanically checked by some static analysis tool. In practice, programmers only write few contracts, mainly preconditions and some object invariants. The reason for that is that other contracts are "clear from the code": Programmers do not like to repeat themselves. As a consequence, any *usable* static verification tool should provide some form of contract inference.

Categories and Subject Descriptors

D [**Software**]: Miscellaneous; D.2.1 [**Software Engineering**]: Requirements/Specifications; D.2.4 [**Software Engineering**]: Software/Program Verification—*Assertion checkers,Programming by contract*

General Terms

Verification

Keywords

Abstract Interpretation,Contracts,Inference

1. CONTRACT INFERENCE

Abstract interpretation [2] provides the theoretical foundations for automatic contracts inference. The contract inference problem can be formulates an abstraction of the trace semantics. For instance, a loop invariant is an abstraction of the states reaching the loop head and an object invariant is an abstraction of all the states reachable in the steady points of an object [8].

1.1 Loop invariants

Abstract interpretation provides an elegant methodology to infer loop invariants. First, set up a sound abstract domain. The abstract domain captures the properties of interest, *e.g.*, the shape of the heap, linear inequalities among program variables [6], or array contents [5]. Soundness guarantees that no concrete behavior is ignored. In practice, the analysis abstract domain is built by composing atomic abstract domains. Second, set up the abstract operations and transfer functions. The abstract operations combine two abstract elements, the transfer functions describe how abstract states are modified by atomic program statements. Third, design convergence operators (widening, narrowing). Convergence operators guarantee that the loop inference process actually terminates.

Finally, the inferred loop invariant is just the abstract element at the loop head computed by the abstract semantics above. In practice, as the loop invariant is mainly used by the tool, we are not interested in having a "nice-looking" invariant.

1.2 Postconditions

Theoretically, an inferred postcondition is similar to a loop invariant: it is just the abstract element at the method return point. However, in practice we'd like to have "nice-looking" and compact postconditions, *e.g.*, without redundant information. At this aim, the postcondition inference proceeds as follows. First, project all the locals from the abstract state — they are not visible to the external callers. Second, ask each atomic abstract domain to serialize its knowledge into a user-readable form — the abstract domains may have a very compact and optimized representation of their elements, not suitable to appear in a contract. Third, remove the contracts that already appear in the source code as postconditions. Fourth, sort and simplify the redundant postconditions.

1.3 Preconditions

We differentiate among *sufficient* and *necessary* preconditions. If valid, a sufficient precondition guarantees the callee is correct, but nothing can be said if it not valid — the callee may or may not be correct. If not-valid, a necessary precondition guarantees the callee is incorrect, but nothing can be said if it is valid. When automatic inference of preconditions is considered, we advocate the inference of necessary precondition. In fact, a sufficient precondition can be too strong for a caller — at worst `false`. On the other hand, a necessary precondition is something that should be satisfied by the

HILT 2013 Nov 10-14 2013, Pittsburgh, PA, USA
ACM ACM 978-1-4503-2466-3/13/11
http://dx.doi.org/10.1145/2527269.2527280 .

caller, otherwise the program will definitely fail later. We designed several algorithms to infer necessary preconditions: atomic, with disjuctions, and for collections [4]. Necessary preconditions can be easily checked to be also sufficient by injecting them and reanalysing the callee [3].

1.4 Object Invariants

We differentiate among *reachable* and *necessary* object invariants. A reachable object invariant characterizes all the fields values that are reachable after the execution of the constructor or any public method in the class [7]. A necessary object invariant is a condition on the object fields that should hold, otherwise there exists a sequence of public method calls causing the object into an error state [1]. Reachable and necessary object invariants are complementary, and both can be used to improve the precision of contract-based static analyzers.

2. CONCLUSIONS

Inferred contracts are vital for the success of verification tools. In our static contract checker, ccheck/Clousot, we spent a large amount of time to implement, refine, and optimize the contract inference algorithms.

3. REFERENCES

[1] M. Bouaziz, L. Logozzo, and M. Fähndrich. Inference of necessary field conditions with abstract interpretation. In *APLAS*, 2012.

[2] P. Cousot and R. Cousot. Abstract interpretation: a unified lattice model for static analysis of programs by construction or approximation of fixpoints. In *POPL'77*. ACM Press, Jan. 1977.

[3] P. Cousot, R. Cousot, M. Fähndrich, and F. Logozzo. Automatic inference of necessary preconditions. In *VMCAI*, pages 128–148, 2013.

[4] P. Cousot, R. Cousot, and F. Logozzo. Contract precondition inference from intermittent assertions on collections. In *VMCAI'11*, 2011.

[5] P. Cousot, R. Cousot, and F. Logozzo. A parametric segmentation functor for fully automatic and scalable array content analysis. In *Proceeding of the 38th ACM Symposium on Principles of Programming Languages (POPL 2011)*. ACM Press, Jan. 2011.

[6] V. Laviron and F. Logozzo. Subpolyhedra: A (more) scalable approach to infer linear inequalities. In *VMCAI '09*, 2009.

[7] F. Logozzo. *Modular static analysis of object-oriented languages*. Thèse de doctorat en informatique, École polytechnique, 2004.

[8] F. Logozzo. Class invariants as abstract interpretation of trace semantics. *Computer Languages, Systems & Structures*, 35(2):100–142, 2009.

SAW: The Software Analysis Workbench

Kyle Carter   Adam Foltzer   Joe Hendrix   Brian Huffman   Aaron Tomb

Galois, Inc
421 SW 6th Avenue, Sauite 300
Portland, OR 97204
{ kcarter, acfoltzer, jhendrix, huffman, atomb }@galois.com

ABSTRACT

Galois has developed a suite of symbolic simulation and formal analysis tools, collectively called the *Software Analysis Workbench* (SAW). SAW provides security analysts and engineers with the ability to generate formal models from C and Java programs and prove properties of those programs using several automated verification tools. SAW is primarily used to verify the correctness of cryptographic implementations, and is able to import specifications written in Cryptol, a language developed by Galois for specifying cryptographic primitives.

In this short paper, we describe the main components of SAW. We then given an overview of the cryptographic implementations that have been verified.

Categories and Subject Descriptors

D.2.3 [**Software Engineering**]: Software/Program Verification—*Correctness proofs*

Keywords

Formal verification, Equivalence checking, Symbolic simulation, JVM, LLVM

1. SOFTWARE ANALYSIS WORKBENCH

In this work, we describe the Software Analysis Workbench (SAW), a set of tools developed at Galois for generating formal models from existing systems code using symbolic simulation. SAW is capable of extracting models from Java code via a symbolic simulator for Java Virtual Machine bytecode, and C code via a symbolic simulator for LLVM bytecode. The primary goal of SAW is to enable developers and security analysts to reason about and prove properties about such programs.

SAW is able to show that a program satisfies a functional specification, and avoids undefined behavior such as accessing invalid memory locations, or dividing by zero. SAW uses automated verification tools including a built-in term rewriter, yices [2], and abc [1] for performing the verification, and users may script multiple verification tactics together in a single problem.

SAW provides multiple interfaces to the simulator tailored to different user needs:

- For Java programmers, SAW provides a command-line symbolic simulator `jss` that mimics the interface to the standard command line interface to the JVM, but enables symbolic execution and allows formal models to be generated.

- For C programmers, SAW provides a command-line symbolic simulator `lss` that takes a linked LLVM bitcode binary compiled with the LLVM `clang` compiler, and runs symbolic simulation to generate formal models. C programmers may control the simulator through a C API.

- Both simulators provide an interactive debugger similar to `gdb` that allows inspecting and modifying simulator state, interactively generating formal models, and understanding third party code.

- Finally, SAW provides *SAWScript*, a scripting language for the tools that allows experts to programmatically generate formal models from code, import formal models from AIG files or Cryptol [3] specifications, do sound compositional verification, and run verification tools.

Internally, SAW uses *symbolic simulation* to build a representation of a programs operations on all execution paths. Although, the number of execution paths in a program may be infinite, it is typically quite small for the cryptographic implications that we have considered. Cryptographic implementations typically contain loops that execute a fixed number of times, and avoid data dependent branches that would expose the cryptographic primitive to advanced key recovery attacks such as timing-based attacks.

As the symbolic simulator evaluates the program, it maps program expressions into *SAWCore*, a dependently-typed formal representation shared by all the tools. SAWCore expressions can be simplified using a built-in rewriter, and then translated into verification formats supported by third party tools such as SMTLIB, AIGER, and (Q)DIMACS.

2. CRYPTOGRAPHIC VERIFICATION

Although SAW can potentially be applied to a wide variety of software, our primary application has been the verification of cryptographic implementations. Cryptographic

HILT'13, November 12–14, 2013, Pittsburgh, PA, USA.
Copyright 2013 ACM 978-1-4503-2467-0/13/11 ...$15.00.
http://dx.doi.org/10.1145/2527269.2527277.

Algorithm	Implementation	LoC	AIG Size	Proof Steps Required	Verification Time
AES-128	Bouncy Castle (Java)	817	1MB	None needed Fully automatic	40 min
SHA-384	libgcrypt (C)	423	3.2MB	12 subspecifications All solved via SAT	160 min
ECDSA (NIST P-384)	galois (Java)	2348	Generation failed More than 5GB	48 subspecifications Multiple solvers used	10 min

Figure 2: Verification of Suite B Implementations

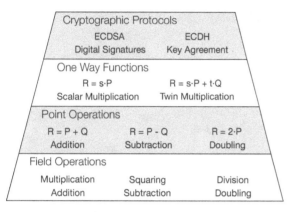

Figure 1: Structure of an Elliptic Curve Cryptographic Implementation

implementations are a critical component of secure systems, and can be quite complex due to the use of low-level implementation tricks and performance optimizations. Current practice is to validate the implementation against random inputs or selected test vectors, but this is incomplete. Not only does testing miss rare bugs, but if the adversary is able to modify the implementation, they could inject bugs that would be highly unlikely to be caught through testing alone.

To reduce the risk of errors in cryptographic implementations, our approach is to use *equivalence checking*, and show that two different implementations of the same algorithm compute the same result on all possible messages and keys. Typically, one of these implementations will be a specification written in Cryptol, and written to closely correspond to the text of the algorithm standard. Cryptol has primitives for different operations that appear bit manipulation, large word arithmetic, and higher order functions to allow algorithms to be specified precisely and clearly. The other implementation is written in C or Java, and designed for efficient execution rather than clarity.

In case studies, we have focused on three different types of cryptographic primitives: (1) symmetric key ciphers such as AES; (2) secure hash functions such as SHA-2; and (3) elliptic curve-based public key algorithms such as ECDSA.

Although our goal is fully automated verification, this has proven to only be tractable on symmetric key ciphers such as AES and DES. We have used SAW to prove functional correctness of different AES implementations from libgcrypt, OpenSSL, and Bouncy Castle with minimal help from the user.

Verification of secure hash functions and public key cryptography requires that the problem be decomposed into multiple verification steps, and compositional techniques to be used to obtain a verification of the whole system. This capa-

bility has been used for verifying libgcrypt's implementation of SHA-2, and a Java implementation of ECDSA signature verification.

For compositional verification, our basic approach is to verify equivalence between low-level operations first, and then use the verification results from low-level operations to simplify the verification of higher-level operations that use the low-level operations. This process may be repeated for algorithms that involve multiple levels.

One of the most complex implementations that we have verified, an implementations of an elliptic curve-based digital signature algorithm for the NIST 384-bit prime field [4], can be viewed as having four layers (see Figure 1 for a depiction of the different algorithms):

1. the lowest layer consists of functions for performing prime field arithmetic;

2. the second layer consists of functions for performing operations on points in an elliptic curve;

3. the third layer contains a one-way scalar multiplication and a twin multiplication designed to efficiently perform two multiplications in parallel;

4. the top layer consists of the top-level digital signature algorithm.

By adopting a compositional approach, one can verify the different algorithms independently and compose the results together.

For comparison purposes, we include a comparison of the work required to verify three different algorithms that are part of the Department of Defense Suite B against corresponding Cryptol specifications. The table in Figure 2 lists the size of each implementation, the number of specifications needed for each method, the tactics used, and the amount of computation time required to run each verification. As the table shows, there is not a clear relationship between the size of the implementation, the number of verification steps, and the time it takes to run a verification effort.

3. CONCLUSIONS

Over the last ten years, enormous progress has been made in scaling up verification towards large systems. The SAW tools are designed for verification of relatively small, critical components written in C and Java. Our main focus is to make verification as automated as current technology can allow, and to support verification of existing programs without requiring modifications to the source during verification.

The SAW toolset could potentially naturally complement Ada-based verification tools such as SPARK, but we have not yet explored how this integration would work. One benefit of such as integration would be to verify third-party C code that could be used with SPARK programs. SPARK could focus on systems-level control code written for a specific application, while the SAW tools would focus on existing code.

4. REFERENCES

[1] R. K. Brayton and A. Mishchenko. ABC: An academic industrial-strength verification tool. In T. Touili, B. Cook, and P. Jackson, editors, *CAV*, volume 6174 of *Lecture Notes in Computer Science*, pages 24–40. Springer, 2010.

[2] B. Dutertre and L. de Moura. Yices 2.0. Available at `http://yices.csl.sri.com/`.

[3] L. Erkök, M. Carlsson, and A. Wick. Hardware/software co-verification of cryptographic algorithms using cryptol. In *FMCAD*, pages 188–191. IEEE, 2009.

[4] National Institute of Standards and Technology. FIPS PUB 186-4: Digital signature standard (DSS), July 2013.

Optimising Verification Effort with SPARK 2014

Pavlos Efstathopoulos
ALTRAN
22 St Lawrence Street
Bath BA1 1AN (United Kingdom)
pavlos.efstathopoulos@altran.com

Andrew Hawthorn
ALTRAN
22 St Lawrence Street
Bath BA1 1AN (United Kingdom)
andrew.hawthorn@altran.com

1. EXTENDED ABSTRACT

The introduction of executable contracts in Ada 2012 brings a new dimension to the debate over which is most efficient: proof or test. The Hi-Lite project was designed to demonstrate the use of executable contracts extension and covered the question of how proven subprograms can reliably call tested subprograms and visa versa. This paper looks at the issue from an industrial perspective to try to identify where it is most efficient to prove or test subprograms.

Test is clearly the most preferred method of verifying software at the moment but the regulated industries have been trying to introduce formal methods ever since software was first written. The acceptance of formal methods seems to be increasing, for example, the latest version of the aerospace standard DO-178 provides explicit guidance on the use of formal methods.

The paper will consider the sorts of questions that need to be asked at the start of a project with respect to choosing and using a programming language and as part of this will introduce the SPARK 2014 language and the capabilities of the SPARK 2014 tool set focusing on the features that support the formal methods supplement of DO-178C. These are the language subset, the use of flow analysis to check for uninitialized, ineffective and unused variables, the use of theorem provers to prove the absence of run-time errors, the use of pre- and post-conditions to specify subprograms and the use of global contracts to check for non-interference between subprograms.

We then briefly walk through relevant aspects of the traditional V-lifecycle explaining how SPARK 2014 can be used as an architectural design tool and specification language as well as a coding language.

With the assumption that SPARK 2014 has been used as a specification language we are now able to decide whether or not to prove, test or use a combination of the two methods to verify our software. We will present examples of the following situations and demonstrate how a combination of proof and test can resolve them all:

1. *Prove by strengthening assertions* - try to fully prove the code by strengthening preconditions and adding assertions until full proof is achieved. No testing is involved in this scenario.

2. *Test without proof* - decide that developing tests is likely to be easier than completing full proof and resort to testing right from the beginning. No proof is involved in this scenario.

3. *Prove some, test some* - attempt to prove the code, find that some verification conditions can not be discharged, and resort to testing. At this point the user can either:

   - perform exclusively testing (prove no properties)
   - or prove only a subset of the properties of the code and test the remaining. For instance, prove freedom of run-time exceptions and test contracts related with functional behaviour.

4. *Use test to debug contracts* - make a first unsuccessful attempt to prove the code and afterwards utilize testing to identify potential issues with the contracts or the implementation. The tests might provide hints as to how the user can alter the code to render it provable. In this scenario, testing reveals the actions that need be performed to achieve full proof.

5. *Contracts can not be written* - not able to formulate a contract, for example, because the subprogram interfaces with an external device that is not modelled.

6. *Proof results not useable* - standards require code to be fully tested. However, as an addition, performing proof could improve the safety case and grant more confidence on the code. In this scenario the user would try to prove as much as possible, but would not insist when proof is too hard. Also, proof of some properties can often be used to support an argument that unit testing of all subprograms is not required.

By walking through the examples, we will demonstrate how a combination of the use of the SPARK 2014 tool set and a commercially available unit testing tool have the potential to dramatically reduce subprogram verification effort.

We conclude by summarising our views on the relative merits of alternative styles of contracts. Specifically, concluding where different types of contracts are most productively used.

Categories and Subject Descriptors

D.2.4 [**Software/Program Verification**]: Formal methods, Programming by contract, Reliability, Validation

General Terms

Design, Reliability, Security, Verification

Keywords

Verification and Validation; Certification; Dependability; DO-178C

Towards The Formalization of SPARK 2014 Semantics With Explicit Run-time Checks Using Coq

Pierre Courtieu,Maria Virginia Aponte,
Tristan Crolard
Conservatoire National des Arts et Metiers
Pierre.Courtieu@cnam.fr,
maria-virginia.aponte_garcia@cnam.fr,
tristan.crolard@cnam.fr

Jerome Guitton
AdaCore
guitton@adacore.com

Zhi Zhang, Robby, Jason Belt,
John Hatcliff
Kansas State University
zhangzhi@ksu.edu, robby@ksu.edu,
belt@ksu.edu, hatcliff@ksu.edu

Trevor Jennings
Altran
trevor.jennings@altran.com

ABSTRACT

We present the first steps of a broad effort to develop a formal representation of SPARK 2014 suitable for supporting machine-verified static analyses and translations. In our initial work, we have developed technology for translating the GNAT compiler's abstract syntax trees into the Coq proof assistant, and we have formalized in Coq the dynamic semantics for a toy subset of the SPARK 2014 language. SPARK 2014 programs must ensure the absence of certain run-time errors (for example, those arising while performing division by zero, accessing non existing array cells, overflow on integer computation). The main novelty in our semantics is the encoding of (a small part of) the run-time checks performed by the compiler to ensure that any well-formed terminating SPARK programs do not lead to erroneous execution. This and other results are mechanically proved using the Coq proof assistant. The modeling of on-the-fly run-time checks within the semantics lays the foundation for future work on mechanical reasoning about SPARK 2014 program correctness (in the particular area of robustness) and for studying the correctness of compiler optimizations concerning run-time checks, among others.

Categories and Subject Descriptors

D.2.4 [**Software Engineering**]: Software/Program Verification, Formal Methods, Correctness Proofs; F.4.1 [**Mathematical Logic and Formal Language**]: Mathematical Logic—*mechanical theorem proving*

General Terms

Reliability, Security, Verification

Keywords

SPARK, Coq Proof Assistant, Formal Semantics, Machine-Verified Proof

1. MOTIVATION

We believe that the certification process of SPARK technology can be stressed by the use of formal semantics. Indeed, the software certification process as required by the DO-178-C [10] standard allows formal verification to replace some forms of testing. This is one of the goals pursued by the SPARK toolchain resulting from the Hi-Lite project [3]. On the other hand, the DO-333 supplement [11] (formal method supplement to DO-178-C) recommends that when using formal methods "all assumptions related to each formal analysis should be described and justified". As any formal static analysis must rely on the behavior of the language being analyzed, a precise and unambiguous definition of the semantics of this language becomes clearly a requirement in the certification process.

We also aim to strengthen the theoretical foundation of the GNAT-prove toolchain. The Ada reference manual [1] introduces the notion of *errors*. These correspond to error situations that must be detected at run time as well as erroneous executions that need not to be detected. In Ada, the former are detected by run-time checks (RTCs) inserted by the compiler. Both must be guaranteed never to occur during the process of proving SPARK (or Ada) subprograms within the GNATprove toolchain [2]. This can be ensured either by static analysis or by generating verification conditions (VCs) showing that the corresponding error situations never occur at that point in the subprogram. The generated VCs must be discharged in order to prove the subprogram. Tools within the GNATprove toolchain strongly rely on the completeness of this VCs generation process. Our semantics setting on top of a proof assistant open the possibility to formally (and mechanically) verify (to some extent) this completeness. In practice, since VCs are actually generated from the RTCs generated by the compiler, this completeness verification amounts to analyzing the RTCs inserted by the compiler in the abstract syntax tree produced by the GNAT compiler.

Finally, one of our long-term goals is to provide infrastructure that can be leveraged in a variety of ways to support machine-verified proofs of correctness of SPARK 2014 static analysis and translations. To this end, we will build a translation framework from SPARK 2014 to Coq, which puts in place crucial infrastructure necessary for supporting formal proofs of SPARK analysis.

Together with the formal semantics of SPARK, it provides the potential to connect to the Compcert [7] certified compiler framework.

2. FORMALIZATION AND PROOF

2.1 SPARK Translation Toolchain

In the long path through the definition of complete semantics for SPARK 2014, a very important step is to build a tool chain allowing the experimentation of the behavior of these semantics on real SPARK 2014 programs. In the front end of this tool chain, as part of the Sireum analysis framework [5], we have developed a tool called Jago [4] that translates XML representation of the GNAT compiler's ASTs into a Scala-based representation in Sireum. This open-source framework enables one to build code translators and analysis tools for SPARK 2014 in Scala. Scala's blending of functional and object-oriented program styles have proven quite useful in other contexts for syntax tree manipulation and analysis. Integrated into Jago is a translation of GNAT ASTs into Coq based representations. In the backend of the tool chain, a certified interpreter encoding run-time checks for the Coq AST has been developed within Coq.

2.2 Formalizing Language Semantics

A major difference between SPARK and other programming languages is that its informal specification as given by the Ada reference manual requires the compiler to detect specific run-time error cases in order to enforce programs robustness. We are currently formalizing the SPARK semantics in Coq that includes run-time checks and working towards adding more language features, such as procedure calls, in our current formalization framework. At this early stage, our formal semantics consider only a small subset of SPARK 2014, and only a small subset of run-time errors. It performs appropriate run-time checks as they are specified by the SPARK and Ada reference manuals. We call these semantics, the *reference semantics*, and we implemented an interpreter certified with respect to them. Thus, our reference semantics can be both manually reviewed by SPARK experts, and also be used to experiment on real source code programs. For those who are interested, we have posted the source code of our formalization on GitHub [6].

2.3 Program Correctness Proof

In Coq, we have formalized a well-formed SPARK program as a well-typed, well-defined and well-checked program. A well-typed program has all its language constructs being consistent with respect to the typing rules and all its variables have correct in/out mode with respect to their reading and writing permissions. A well-defined program is a program with all its used variables initialized. A well-checked program is a program having the appropriate checks inserted at the correct places in AST trees. It is proved that for all well-formed SPARK programs in our formalized language subset, they will execute as we expect and will never exhibit undefined behavior.

3. RELATED WORK

Formal semantics were previously defined for SPARK Ada 83 in [8, 9]. This definition includes both the static and the dynamic semantics of the language and rely on a precise notation inspired by the Z notation. Formalizing the full SPARK subset was clearly a challenging task and the result is indeed quite impressive: more than 500 pages were required for the complete set of rules. However, these semantics were not executable (it was only given on paper) and no tool was used to check the soundness of the definition. Moreover, no property was proved using these semantics, and more importantly, run-time checks were only considered as side conditions on semantics rules without being formally described.

4. CONCLUSION AND FUTURE WORK

We have implemented a prototype tool chain from SPARK 2014 language subset to Coq and its semantical formalization and proof in Coq. The experiments on running the certified interpreter shows that our formalized SPARK semantics can capture the desired run-time behavior. This is encouraging, however there is still a lot of work needed to be done.

Our next step is to prove the correctness of optimizations that remove useless run-time checks. Our interpreted semantics are parameterized by the set of run-time checks to be performed. These semantics may be called with an incomplete set of run-time checks, and can evaluate in that case to an erroneous execution. A future work could be to formalize some optimizations actually performed by the GNAT compiler, and remove those useless run-time checks. The idea would be to prove these optimizations correct, namely to prove that those executions with *less* run-time checks behave exactly as those following the reference semantics, which perform systematically *all* the checks.

In addition, we are also interested in adding more SPARK language features, such as procedure calls, pre/post aspects and loop invariants, to expand our current SPARK subset and make it more practical. This work on formalizing the SPARK semantics also paves the way for our further work on machine-verified proof of correctness of SPARK static analysis and translation tools.

Acknowledgements

The authors would like to thank Emmanuel Polonowski and Yannick Moy for their valuable comments and suggestions on this work.

5. REFERENCES

[1] Ada reference manual.
    http://www.ada-auth.org/standards/ada12.html.
[2] Adacore Gnatprove tool.
    http://www.open-do.org/projects/hi-lite/gnatprove/.
[3] Adacore Hi-Lite project.
    http://www.open-do.org/projects/hi-lite/.
[4] Jago translation tool.
    https://github.com/sireum/bakar/tree/master/sireum-bakar-jago.
[5] Sireum software analysis platform. http://www.sireum.org.
[6] Source code for SPARK 2014 language subset formalization.
    https://github.com/sireum/bakar/tree/master/sireum-bakar-formalization.
[7] X. Leroy. Formal verification of a realistic compiler. *Communications of the ACM*, 52(7):107–115, 2009.
[8] W. Marsh. Formal semantics of SPARK - static semantics, Oct 1994.
[9] I. O'Neill. Formal semantics of SPARK - dynamic semantics, Oct 1994.
[10] RTCA DO-178. Software considerations in airborne systems and equipment, 2011.
[11] RTCA DO-333. Formal methods supplement to do-178c and do-278a, 2011.

Real-Time Programming on Accelerator Many-Core Processors

Stephen Michell
Maurya Software Inc
Canada
stephen.michell@maurya.on.ca

Brad Moore
General Dynamics
Canada
brad.moore@gdcanada.com

Luís Miguel Pinho
CISTER/INESC-TEC, ISEP
Portugal
lmp@isep.ipp.pt

ABSTRACT

Multi-core platforms are challenging the way software is developed, in all application domains. For the particular case of real-time systems, models for the development of parallel software must be able to be shown correct in both functional and non-functional properties at design-time. In particular, issues such as concurrency, timing behaviour and interaction with the environment need to be addressed with the same caution as for the functional requirements.

This paper proposes an execution model for the parallelization of real-time software, based upon a fine-grained parallelism support being proposed to Ada, a programming language particularly suited to the development of critical, concurrent software. We also show the correctness of the proposed model in terms of satisfying constraints related to execution order and unbounded priority inversions.

Categories and Subject Descriptors

D.3.3 [**Programming Languages**]: Language Constructs and Features – *Concurrent programming structures.*

Keywords

Multi-core; real-time; programming language; Ada; dispatching domains

1. INTRODUCTION

The importance of parallel computations has grown significantly as the trend to use multi-core and many-core platforms spreads to new application domains, and parallelization is the only means to continue to be able to support increasingly complex software in hardware architectures which no longer evolve to faster speeds. We are thus witnessing an immense growth in parallel programming methodologies and models, put forward to address the inherent complexity of developing reliable software on these platforms.

This is the case even for domains which are traditionally more conservative in evolving to new hardware or software models, such as real-time applications. In this domain, systems are built in such a way as to guarantee at design time both functional behaviour, and timing behaviour in addition to other constraints. These systems present significant challenges to the development of applications, as they require the guarantee of predictable timing behaviour as they interact with, and react to, the external environment.

To meet these challenges, models and technologies incorporate intrinsically the notion of time, priorities and concurrency. Programming models therefore need to be based in languages which integrate these notions, and any solution to the development of parallel software must adhere to the same requirements. Any approach which considers parallelization must be rigorous and amenable to verification.

Within this context, it is necessary to address the integration of fine-grained parallelism in the Ada programming language [9]. Ada's sound specification of concurrency is based on the direct support for tasks, supporting coarse-grain multi-core programming.

A fine-grain parallel model for Ada has recently been proposed [13], based on the notion of tasklets, which are non schedulable computation units (similar to Cilk [8] or OpenMP [12] "tasks"). Tasklets may be executed by a pool of worker tasks.

This paper starts from this existent work [13] to propose a model of execution for the parallelization of real-time software based upon a separation of domains for the execution of the application tasks and the execution of their parallel components. The tasks of the application are executed in a single core, while the remaining cores are used as accelerators, to execute parallel code blocks on behalf of the application tasks. We also show analytically that the model can preserve important properties of such systems, such as avoidance of unbounded priority inversions, deadlocks[4] and race conditions. Further work is needed to include analysis of timing properties, including issues such as contention for common busses and shared global state.

This work contrasts with other work on scheduling real-time tasks in multi-core systems (in [7] the reader will find a survey of the major directions being followed and approaches being proposed). In contrast to other proposals for parallel real-time tasks [6][11][17][2]) this approach tends to be much simpler and maintains the structure, methodologies, code, and verification techniques currently being used for real-time systems while providing extra processing power when needed in a less intrusive way.

Presently Ada does not have the necessary syntax and libraries to support the proposals given here. Paraffin [14][15] implements a set of generics which can already be used to achieve the results of [13], but require more explicit rearrangement of loops and function calls than can be done with dedicated syntax.

The paper is structured as follows. The next section provides the required background, which is then further detailed in Section 3 for the case of real-time programming models. Section 4 then provides some definitions, while Section 5 describes the ongoing work to address parallelism within Ada. Section 6 describes the model of computation and shows its correctness. Section 7 is conclusions and Future work. An annex is also included to show a complete example.

2. BACKGROUND
2.1 Brief Summary of Real-Time Systems
Real-time systems are systems in which some or all events in the system must result in the correct response within a bounded fixed time interval [4]. Real-time systems are usually divided into 2 domains. Soft real-time systems are ones where some calculations can exceed expected time (i.e. the system can accommodate some slippage). Hard real-time systems are characterized by the property that all of the bounds on calculations are absolute – i.e., a late answer is as bad as no answer or a wrong answer, and an early answer can also be problematic. Some examples of real-time systems are industrial processing systems, transportation systems such as airplane control, train braking systems and communication, such as network controllers for wifi and ethernet controllers.

Real-time programming presents significant challenges even for single-CPU programming. It is event driven, feedback-oriented, time critical in that:

- important calculations have "best before" (for soft real-time), "must before" and "not before" (for hard real-time) times; and

- they are highly concurrent with a minimum of interrupt routines, event routines, and likely tasks (threads) to handle natural concurrency that occurs.

In order to work with such systems, a notion of priority (imperativeness) is an important concept to ensure that the most imperative calculations are done in preference to other calculations, and to maintain schedulability (i.e. to meet the hard real-time deadlines for the critical tasks). Priority is so important that all CPU's have a notion of priority embedded in the hardware to control which classes of hardware get preferential service when conflict exists, and all operating systems and run times have a notion of software priority that extends the hardware priority right down to the "idle task".

A large real-time program may have:

- Interrupt handlers delivering external I/O to the system;

- Clock handlers managing time and making decisions about time;

- Event handlers working with "softer" events with high software priority but low hardware priority;

- Worker tasks interacting with sets of interrupt and event handlers;

- Calculation engines maintaining real-world properties, such as velocity, position, acceleration; and

- Managers managing system state, task states and modes.

Such a program uses time, priority and programmed state to schedule and manage the interaction of the multitude of system components to keep the system functioning safely, securely and correctly. The precise interaction of many components is vital to that correct functioning [10].

2.2 Introduction of Parallel Computation
Like all other domains, the real-time computation domain has been demanding more and more CPU power to solve its problems, as new applications such as vision systems are introduced, very large data sets are processed, and more fidelity is demanded of calculations. To date, almost all real-time systems have resided on single CPUs [10], or if using multiple CPUs, have highly restricted the ways that they can interact so that the constraints of the real-time domain can be satisfied. The stagnation in the growth of CPU speed means that real-time systems must seriously consider how they can make use of multi-core and many-core systems.

Even real-time systems sometimes need a bigger calculation window than can be delivered by a single CPU in the time constraints available, such as processing vision system frames to detect and identify obstacles. Many calculations are approximate, and increasing the processor power increases the fidelity of the calculation (and permits some complex algorithms that may not be permissible on a single CPU). Dividing the calculation across multiple cores permits increased calculation efficiency, provided that it can integrate into real-time systems constraints.

To satisfy the constraints, one must verify before the system is fielded that it will operate correctly always, that all eventualities have been considered and that all corner cases have been considered. Typical approaches are static verification-based analysis at design time that may include formal verification, Worst Case Execution Time (WCET) analysis, Worst Case Response Time (WCRT), measurement, modelling, and extensive human review.

Multi-core systems dramatically change the way that components interact with each other and with the external world in that:

- Tasks executing on separate cores often have very different access to memory, network, busses and registers, interfering with each other via those covert resources;

- Some hardware or interrupts may not be available on all CPU's;

- Memory access may be orders of magnitude slower, depending upon locality of reference and cache issues; and

- Objects such as spin locks may give (unintended) preferential treatment to some cores or tasks. So, although multi-core systems are assumed to be homogenous, bottlenecks such as memory bus speeds and number of cores trying to access common memory are leading to non-homogeneous systems, such as CC-NUMA.

The items discussed above simply add to the complication that multiprocessing systems already present to any previously sequential algorithm.

3. DEFINITIONS

Task – in Ada is both a unit of design mapping of concurrency and unit of concurrent execution. In terms of execution model, tasks are similar to threads in POSIX. In fact they are typically mapped to OS threads unless accompanied by a specialized runtime.

Application Task (AT) – A task that is declared by the programmer. Application tasks are declared to be in a single domain that, in this example, execute on a single processor. All real-time ATs have a unique priority that is higher than any non-real-time application task. An application task with priority i is labelled AT_i.

Parallelism OPportunity (POP) – The place in an application where sequential code can be executed by parallel units (but is not mandated to be executed in parallel).

Dispatching Policy – The policy which governs the allocation and scheduling behaviour of tasks on specific processors.

Dispatching Domain – a named set of CPUs within which tasks assigned to that domain are scheduled according to the dispatching policy for that domain.

Worker Task – A task that belongs to a task pool and executes parallel code on behalf of an AT at a POP. All q worker tasks $WT_i(1..q)$ of a dedicated task pool service a single application task AT_i. In this model, all WT_i execute on a specific dispatching domain.

Spawn – To create an object representing a parallel code unit and submitting it to be processed by a worker task.

4. PARALLEL ADA MODEL PROPOSAL

Having identified the lack of direct support for use of fine-grained parallelism in Ada, we recently proposed a mechanism that the programmer can use and precisely control fine-grain parallelism in loops and subroutine calls [13]. The basic mechanism leverages from the new Ada (2012) aspects syntax to permit an aspect "with parallel" to suggest to the compiler that work be parallelized across processors, together with a set of library package interfaces to support user-defined or user-augmented fine-grained parallelism.

In order to effectively describe the new concurrent behaviour, this work introduced a unit of parallelism called a "tasklet" (similar to the Cilk concept of task). Unlike Ada tasks, tasklets are not nameable or directly visible in a program. A tasklet carries the execution of a subprogram or of a code fragment (such as part of a "for" loop) in parallel with other tasklets executing the same code fragment (with different state) and possibly in parallel with other tasklets executing code fragments from other Ada tasks.

This proposal incorporates logical units of parallelism in the semantic model of the language, allowing potential parallelism to be expressed both for task/control parallelism, where the control structures of the code (e.g. loops and subprograms) which are amenable to parallelization are identified, and for data parallelism where data structures (arrays or records) are potentially processed in parallel, based on the notion of a logical unit of parallelism.

The programmer identifies these potential parallel opportunities in the code, guiding the compiler in generating code that creates the logical tasklets. During execution, the runtime executes the tasklets in parallel, if the load of the system allows it. These tasklets may actually not exist as runtime identifiable objects (it depends on actual compiler and libraries implementation) but exist as logical entities of the program. Note that this model also allows integrating vectorization, as logically the compiler can decompose parallel processing in several tasklets which are directly executed in hardware.

There are two types of tasklets. The first is created by the compiler when it can determine that an operation can be parallelized and submitted to multiple processors, and hence is not visible to the programmer. Usages of this could include default initialization, assignment of values to arrays of records, copying large structures using the Ada assignment operator, or compiler identifiable parallelizable loops, as shown in Figure 1.

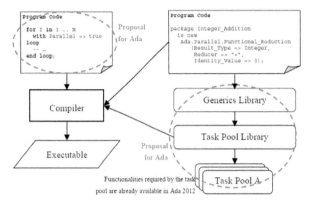

Figure 1 - Proposal for Tasklets in Ada 2012 [13]

The second tasklet type is created by the compiler upon instruction from the programmer, who uses explicit syntax to guide the compiler and runtime in deciding how much parallelism should be provided (e.g. by "chunking"), and whether the tasklets should process work bundles using a work-sharing, work-seeking[1] or work-stealing model. The syntax includes the use of aspects on subprograms and loops.

Tasklets are meant to augment, not replace tasking as the unit of concurrency. Programmers will declare an intent that code fragments be executable in parallel, but do not necessarily concern themselves with the details of the parallelism itself, or how it interoperates with other tasks. They can, however, as we will show, extend the syntax and add runtime mechanisms to achieve specific concurrency behaviours.

Each tasklet behaves as if it were executed by a single Ada task that was explicitly created for the execution of the tasklets and terminated immediately after execution of the code fragment. In order to make tasklets integrate smoothly with the tasking mechanism, priority, and real-time bounds, tasklets can be executed by worker tasks. The Ada tasking model is then used to express the concurrency since tasks in Ada already have a computationally sound model that addresses the issues (i.e. proven support for real-time systems) raised here. To not base this

---

[1] Work seeking is similar to work stealing, but the worker with extra work participates directly in process by frequently checking to see if idle workers are available and offering work directly to the idle worker. We believe (but have not confirmed) that work seeking is safe from priority inversions. See [14][15].

concurrency on tasks puts at risk the priority model of Ada for any real-time programs.

In a generic system the compiler is free to create as many tasks as it needs to execute tasklet code, and any such tasks that execute tasklets are not visible to application code. This can be augmented with user-defined pools of tasks to execute tasklet code by matching the interface that the compiler exposes; a set of packages and generics to let the pool provide the service.

4.1 Syntax

The most obvious opportunities for parallelism are the subprogram call and the loop. For a subprogram call one can declare to the compiler the desire to execute the subprogram in parallel with its caller by writing

```
A_Value :=  Some_Function(Value1) with Parallel
               + Some_Function(Value2);
```

Here the subprogram `Some_Function(Value2)` will be executed in parallel with `Some_Function(Value1)` and the caller waits at a point before its return value is consumed by the "+" operation [2].

For loops the basic syntax is

```
for I in Integer 1..N with Parallel loop
   -- some calculation on I
end loop;
```

or if we wanted to control chunking of the algorithm (say to split among C cores using work-sharing)

```
for I in integer 1..N
        with Parallel, Chunk_Size => N/C
loop
   -- some calculation on I
end loop;
```

More details can be found on [13] on the syntax and how issues such as managing complex calculations that need reduction, identity values, and other tuning parameters, are addressed.

Using the same model, data-level parallelism can be supported by allowing the notion of potentially parallel data types, where operations can be parallelized (operations in data types are actually subprograms). These data types can have the operations overridden by specifying "with Parallel => true" and what would be the parallelizable units.

In this model, the compiler is free to optimize and use SIMD hardware when available (as it already can), but may also generate logical tasklets, within the same generic model as above, and share the same task pools.

For instance, the following example describes a simple parallel array, which the compiler can vectorize in some architectures:

```
-- this can be vectorized
type Par_Arr is array 1 .. 100 of Integer
  with Parallel => true;
function "+"(Left, Right: Par_Arr) return Par_Arr
  with Parallel_By_Element =>
              function "+" (Left, Right: Integer)
                               return Integer;
```

---

[2]   We also permit the "with Parallel" aspect to be placed on the subprogram specification, letting all calls to execute in parallel with the caller. In this case one would need "with Parallel => False" to prohibit it from happening.

For more complex data types, the model would be the same:

```
type My_Type is record
   -- whatever
end record;

function "+"(Left, Right: My_Type) return My_Type;
-- implements addition of two My_Type objects

type My_Type_Arr is array 1 .. 100 of My_Type
   with Parallel => true;

function "+"(Left, Right: My_Type_Arr)
   return My_Type_Arr
   with Parallel_By_Element =>
              function "+" (Left, Right: My_Type)
                              return My_Type,
        Chunk_Size => 50;

   -- any "+" operation on My_Type_Arr can be
   -- parallelized by compiler
   -- even automatically vectorized when possible

function "*"(Left, Right: My_Type_Arr)
   return My_Type is  -- this cannot be
                              by_element
begin
   -- implement dot product with parallel loop
end "*";
```

Aspects could be allowed on the statement of execution to control the level of chunking to perform, either in the specification of the type, or in the actual code performing the operation:

```
My_Arr_1, My_Arr_2: My_Type_Arr;
-- ...
... My_Arr_1 + My_Arr_2 with  Parallel,
                              Chunk_Size => 10;
```

Assignment into a parallel data type could be automatically parallelized by the compiler using the same context as the parallel operation being performed (or freely if no other operation was being performed). Note that for expressions, a "with Parallel" gives instructions to the compiler to parallelize as much as possible. If the programmer wishes finer control of the parallelization of the operations and subprograms she may need to rewrite the expression. Further research is needed on the best suitable approach for this finer control.

4.2 Facilities for Programmer-defined Task Pools

The examples given above are enough to have the compiler generate a set of parallel dispatches to tasks or processors to execute their work component and return partial results for final reduction. Many situations exist, however, in which more control is needed, such as when the priority of the application task requires a set of worker tasks with the same priority. Therefore, there are times when the application needs to define its own task pool, and to have the compiler invoke these explicit worker tasks. In order to integrate the worker tasks, there needs to be an interface between the worker tasks and the application program.

This interface is provided by the addition of package `Ada.Parallel` together with a set of child packages to the Ada runtime library to support user-defined or user-augmented fine-grained parallelism. This library contains interfaces to mechanisms (among other things) to support the creation of task pools to permit the dispatching of fine-grained parallel work to user-written pools of worker tasks, and parallel manager objects to control exactly how the parallel work is to be dispatched and controlled. The details of this work can be found in [13] and [16].

The Ada.Parallel interfaces also include generic packages to implement function reducers and loop iterators that are shown in [13] as well as work plans to permit work to be processed by a much smaller number of processors (and tasks) than there are work packages to be done. For example, load balancing may improve performance in some situations but not in others. Thus, user-defined task pools can be created to satisfy specialized dispatch conditions, such as a bounded set of worker tasks, or set priority for all worker tasks, or even a set of Ravenscar [3] compliant tasks for very specialized runtimes.

Let us return to the basic syntax to invoke a tasklet, with parallel. In order to access the user-defined task pools, we need more machinery. Here detailed aspects can be used for that purpose.

```
for I in 1 .. 1000
     with Parallel          => True,
          Worker_Count      => 10,
          Parallel_Manager  =>
                    WSL.Work_Sharing_Manager,
          Task_Pool         => My_Worker_Pool,
          Chunk_Size        => 100,
          Priority          =>
                    System.Priority'Last,
          Load_Sensitive    => True
loop
     --...
end loop;
```

In the example above, WSL.Work_Sharing_Manager [4] is a user-defined package that is an instantiation of a generic child package of Ada.Parallel [16].

An important point to note is that the communication between the application task that contains the POP and the worker tasks that execute the tasklets is always via an Ada protected object(s). Such protected objects obey the ceiling priority protocol [4], which means that priority-based scheduling is supported by sound scheduling theory. It is also important to note that worker task pools can be assigned to domains that match characteristics of the hardware [3], whether it be a few multi-cores in a homogenous environment or a many-core system without shared memory.

5. THE ACCELERATOR MODEL – A POTENTIAL FOR REAL-TIME MULTI-CORE SYSTEMS

Building on this existent work, this section presents a model for real-time programming for multi-core and many-core processors, using available cores as accelerators of the real-time application tasks. We also present a couple of examples of alternative constructions of a real-time program that follows our model and shows how a real-time analysis of such a program could be undertaken.

For our real-time system model, we propose a system where all application tasks execute on a single core using the priority mechanism and communicate with each other and with interrupts and events via protected objects that obey the ceiling priority protocol (e.g. with FIFO spinning [5] or other applicable protocol). We assume that every application task has a unique priority to express its degree of urgency, and that the priority of all real-time tasks is higher than the priority of non-real-time tasks. For normal inter-task interactions, each protected object shared by two or more tasks has a priority equal to the highest priority task that can call a protected subprogram or entry of the object [5].

For our system, we assume that there are P tasks with unique priorities $1..P$ (as in Ada higher numbers indicate higher priority), called application task $1..P$ and denoted $AT_1 .. AT_p$. Furthermore, for the examples below, we assume that task AT_1 and AT_2 need more computational power than is available from the first core, but we have M (in the examples below $M=7$) additional cores available. We now show two different configurations for distributing the work and show how the real-time properties of the program are preserved for each configuration.

5.1 Mapping 1 – Independent Worker Dispatching Domains

The first mapping (Figure 2) is used when each application task AT_i ($\forall i \in 1..P$) is assigned a non-overlapping subset of the M accelerator cores, within a AT_i-specific worker dispatching domain. In the example, we create three dispatching domains, AD, WD_1 and WD_2, where AD contains core 1 upon which all AT tasks execute. Dispatching domain WD_2 contains 3 cores and has a task pool containing 3 (or more) [6] worker tasks $WT_2(1..3)$, each at priority 2, the same as AT_2. The communication between AT_2 and $WT_2(1..3)$ occurs via work manager protected object 2 ($WMPO_2$) with a ceiling priority of 2. Similarly, AT_1 is supported by dispatching domain WD_1 consisting of 4 cores and a task pool containing 4 worker tasks $WT_1(1..4)$, and communication between AT_1 and $WT_1(1..4)$ occurs via $WMPO_1$.

When AT_i ($i=1$ or 2 in the example) dispatches work to its worker tasks, e.g. using

```
for j in 1..N with Parallel => XXX loop,
```

AT_i calls a protected procedure of $WMPO_i$ to schedule up to N worker tasks and then spin-waits for a final result. Worker tasks $WT_i(1..q)$ iteratively collect a work packet, calculate a result, return the result, until all work packets have completed and a final answer can be returned. At this point, AT_i is unblocked and

---

[3]   The Ravenscar Tasking Profile is a highly restrictive subset of Ada tasking with fixed priority tasks that can only be statically declared and that communicate by protected objects that can only have a single entry with a single queue element.
[4]   WSL refers to Work_Sharing_Loops.

[5]   The model and arguments provided herein rely upon the fact that all application tasks execute on a single CPU and rely upon the ceiling priority protocol to let correctness calculations be performed. If work is distributed to worker tasks in other cpu's, and these worker tasks cannot communicate or share variables with worker tasks from other applications, then they have no dependency with each other outside of the application tasks.
[6]   It may permissible to create more tasks in a single pool than there are available CPUs. All can be dispatched by a "with Parallel" call and will sort themselves out to do the calculation. Some mechanisms, such as work sharing, may have better efficiency when there are more tasks than CPUs.

returns with its result. In our model, parallelizable code cannot share resources with other application tasks. This means that worker tasks will not share resources between domains.

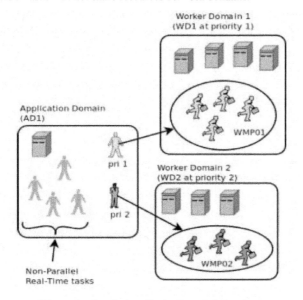

Figure 2 - Real-time Tasks Parallelizing in Dedicated Worker Domains

The challenge is to show that real-time schedulability and analyzability of the application are preserved. For example, we need to show an absence of priority inversion where for priority(i)>priority(j), an AT_i is ready to execute but cannot because an AT_j is executing (excluding cases where AT_j is calling a protected operation with priority >priority(i)).

By priority rules, AT_j can only execute when all higher priority tasks are waiting on a suspend, block or delay operation. It may be interrupted while it is doing its work, but cannot interrupt any $AT_i(3..P)$ except when calling a protected object to communicate with some AT_i. Without loss of generality, in the example, AT_2 can be interrupted when scheduling work for $WT_2(1..3)$ because $WMPO_2$ has priority 2, and can be interrupted by all higher priority tasks.

When AT_2 has dispensed all of its work, and $WT_2(1..3)$ interacts with $WMPO_2$, all interactions occur within the processor of each WT_2 task and therefore do not impact AT_i, $i>2$. Even when the work has completed and AT_i must do some computation in $WMPO_2$, the priority is such that higher priority tasks always get service.

The argument made above for AT_2 applies also to AT_1, except that AT_2 is now added to the set of application tasks that cannot be blocked by AT_1 or its $WT_1(1..4)$. Now however, we must also consider interactions between $WT_2(1..3)$ and $WT_1(1..4)$. There is none, because each belongs on independent dispatching domains, there is no sharing of data between parallel opportunities in the AT_i and AT_j, and even the execution of $WMPO$ code called by worker tasks is independent because of the independent domains.

5.2 Mapping 2 – Shared Worker Domain

The second mapping (Figure 3) considers the case where we only create a single worker domain of M cores and map all WT task pools to this WD domain. We further permit any AT requiring

tasklets to be somewhere in the range of tasks, not necessarily only the lowest.

In order to accomplish their work, application tasks make liberal use of tasklets implemented by pools of worker tasks executing in the single dispatching domain (WD) that contains all remaining processors. For this example we change the previous scenario by placing worker tasks into a single worker task domain, but here we permit the notion that application tasks at any priority can use tasklets. We continue to show for the example only AT_1 and AT_2 using worker tasks but the analysis and verification is generalized for all combinations.

In this case, when 2 or more application tasks compete for resources and they are at different priorities then all worker tasks for each task will compete on the multi-core domain with the same priority rules, meaning that all tasks for the highest priority work will receive computing resources, and lower priority worker tasks will only proceed when there are more available cores in WD than there are higher priority tasks left to execute.

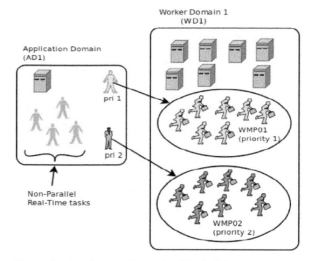

Figure 3 - Accelerator Example - Single Worker Domain

For this model, we assume that there are N cores and $M=N-1$ cores in WD. Without loss of generality we consider 2 arbitrary application tasks, AT_i and AT_j. We further assume that priority(AT_i) > priority(AT_j). Each AT_i (and AT_j) has a set of dedicated worker tasks $WT_i(1..Q<N-1)$ and $WT_j(1..R<N-1)$ and each communicates through its dedicated work manager protected object $WMPOi$ and $WMPOj$. We further assume that

$$priority(WMPO_i) = priority(AT_i) = priority(WT_i),$$

and similarly for AT_j, WT_j and $WMPO_j$. We assume that AT_i and AT_j spin-wait on completion of worker tasks. We also discuss implications when $AT_{i,j}$ are free to block.

We claim that this scenario does not introduce priority inversions (i.e. it never happens that AT_i or any worker task $WT_i(q)$ is ready to execute but cannot because either AT_j or $WT_j(r)$ occupies a processor) [7].

---

[7] The notion of priority inversion can only be applied on a single dispatching domain. If a task T_i, $i>j$ is ready to run in domain D_1 and T_j is executing domain D_2, this is a design decision, not a priority inversion.

5.3 Verification

Assumptions

- All tasks, by the nature of Ada protected objects when supported by the Ada real-time annex, and configured to use the ceiling priority protocol, follow the ceiling priority rules. This means that all communication between application tasks happens through protected operations at a priority higher than the highest priority task that uses them. This also means that all nested interactions occur at increasing levels of priority. Priority rules guarantee deadlock freedom and absence of unbounded priority inversion, in a single core [4].

- All real-time application tasks (AT) have a unique CPU priority and we label each AT_i by its priority i and the lowest priority real-time task has priority greater than the highest priority non-real-time task. This is to guarantee that they complete their task in bounded time, which accounts for the total time taken by higher priority tasks.

- All real-time AT_i execute in a dispatching domain that consists of a single core, relying upon priority to give the most urgent task the processor, and relying upon tasklets to perform CPU-intensive calculations while application tasks spin-wait for results. We nevertheless present a case (8a) where this is relaxed and application tasks may suspend.

- Each AT_i that requires additional computational power has a bounded dedicated pool of worker tasks WT to implement the tasklets. It also has a dedicated protected object (or set of protected objects in the case of a Ravenscar implementation of this model). We label WT for AT_i as $WT_i(1..q)$ and they have the same priority in WD as AT_i has in AD.

- AT_i and AT_j do not share memory resources except via protected objects. Also $WT_i(1..q)$ and $WT_j(1..r)$ do not share memory resources.

- Spawning tasklets to worker tasks is not allowed in protected objects and no potentially blocking operations are called from any WT_i. Note that this limits considerably the model and in particular prevents the use of blocking mechanisms when implementing nested or divide-and conquer parallelism. It provides a safer model for analysis at the expense of restricting parallelism. In domains where it is acceptable, these restrictions may be relaxed to allow for instance workers to spin-wait for the results of another worker, which would allow more efficient and expressive parallelism.

- All $WT_i(1..q)$ execute in a single dispatching domain that includes all of the remaining cores after the allocation of the application task core. The model is independent of WT_i being allowed or not to migrate within the cores of the domain. However, the analysis focuses on the case where WT_i tasks are statically assigned to cores.

- Non-real-time priority tasks may share the application task domain, if already foreseen in the application, but will not share the worker task dispatching domains. These tasks will execute with priorities lower than those of the real-time application tasks hence will not interfere with the progress of work for these tasks. Any communication between real-time and non-real-time tasks needs to be performed in a controlled and correct way, as it would already need to be (independently of the model here proposed), and cannot occur while real-time tasks are in a parallelized region.

- The worker task domain manager (*WTDM*) for each application task contains the protected object(s) $WMPO_i$ used for communication between AT_i and $WT_i(1..q)$. This protected object has the same priority as does the AT_i and WT_i that communicate through it.

- The blocking model for application tasks waiting for replies from worker tasks is spin waiting at the priority of AT_i.

- All WCET calculations for each application task and worker tasks are determined as usual and include preemptions, migration, communications time, cache misses, bus contention.

Claim

No priority inversion is introduced by the model – i.e. there will be no task AT_i ready to run with work with no available core while AT_j, $i>j$ and *priority(i)>priority(j)*, is executing. Similarly there will be no task WT_i ready to run with no available core while task WT_j is executing.

Proof: Break into cases.

Case 1 – application task AT_i is executing and has not initiated any work for $WT_i(1..q)$. By priority rules on the single core, task AT_j cannot be executing.

Case 2 – application task AT_i is calling the work management PO ($WMPO_i$), setting up the Q<N-1 work items for workers. Task AT_j is on the same core as AT_i and cannot be executing by priority rules.

Case 3 – task AT_i is spin-waiting on the return of results. Task AT_j cannot commence execution.

Case 4 – Task AT_j is executing but has not reached a Parallel Opportunity and AT_i is resumed. AT_j is preempted and AT_i executes, spawns its worker tasks, collects results, and finishes. AT_j then completes execution, scheduling its worker tasks, collecting results and completing.

Case 5 – AT_i does not schedule to execute in this scenario and AT_j wakes up, calls $WMPO_j$ and schedules $WT_j(1..r)$ on WD. The WT_j complete, return values and AT_j proceeds back to a suspend state.

Case 6 – AT_j executes, initiates worker tasks $WT_j(1..r)$, then spin-waits for its workers to complete. While AT_j is spinning, AT_i commences execution, preempts AT_j, initiates $WT_i(1..q)$ and spins waiting on results. In a shared domain, $WT_i(1..q)$ will preempt some or all $WT_j(1..r)$ and all proceed to completion, releasing AT_i to finish its calculations. While AT_i is finishing its calculations, $WT_j(1..r)$ workers have resumed. Once AT_i completes, then AT_j resumes spinning for its results, which may or may not already be there.

Case 7 – AT_i and AT_j have initiated worker tasks and AT_i is spin waiting for a result with AT_j preempted still in the protected object $WMPO_j$. $WT_i(1..q)$ complete, with the last one releasing AT_i. AT_j continues to be preempted on $WMPO_j$ waiting for the completion of $WT_j (1..r)$. $WT_j(1..r)$ execute while AT_i executes on the application domain core. If some or all $WT_j(1..r)$ complete before AT_i finishes, they try to access a protected procedure of $WMP0_j$ to deposit their results, but cannot acquire the protected object, since AT_j has not released it. After AT_i finishes execution, then AT_j exits $WMP0_j$ and spin-waits on the results from $WT_j(1..r)$. $WT_j(1..r)$ acquire $WMP0_j$

to deposit their results. Once all WT_j $(1..r)$ complete, then AT_j is released.

Case 8 – same as case 6, except that $WT_i(1..q)$ do not use all cores, or as $WT_i(1..q)$ complete, cores are released and all $WT_j(1..r)$ complete before all $WT_i(1..q)$ complete. At this point AT_j is freed the next time that it checks for completed work, but the spinning of AT_i does not let this happen until all $WT_i(1..q)$ complete and AT_i completes and blocks for the next release. AT_j then continues.

If we permit blocking by AT_i (i.e. self-suspend waiting for $WT_i(1..q)$ to complete instead of spin-waiting), then the following additional cases exist (Note that the system will not be ICPP compliant but some real-time systems analysis permits blocking by tasks in more than one place):

Case 8a – same as Case 8 except that AT_j is free to execute upon release as AT_i is blocked waiting on the WT_i to complete. AT_j may or may not finish its iteration before AT_i is released. Spawning tasklets inside a protected object is not allowed, thus we are guaranteed that AT_i is not using any resources when suspending.

The discussion and analysis above only shows that there is no structural contention that could cause deadlock or introduce priority inversions. It does not address platform-specific issues such as bus contention, DMA contention, cache-flush/cache-miss issues, or local memory/global memory access times: all of which are critical issues for real-time systems. Such analysis is the subject of several current (and future) research works.

The discussion also does not discuss the role of high priority real-time tasks that share the application domain but do not use tasklets. These tasks are the highest priority tasks that interact with the external environment but consume few processor cycles (e.g. Interrupt handlers). If such a task AT_i preempts an executing application task that has not yet called its $WMPO_i$, processing happens normally. If it is preempted while a call to $WMPO_i$ is in progress, the priority rules mean that the call waits until the preempting operation completes, as would happen in a single CPU system. If the higher priority task executes in the application domain while WT_i are executing, AT_i is preempted so no interruption occurs, and the processing of any returned values waits until the higher priority task completes.

The model above was chosen specifically to closely match the existing knowledge base and verification approaches for real-time programs based on single CPUs and priority to control scheduling. The extension of the single core to a worker domain that matches the main single core extends the priority model to the worker tasks. The choice of a dedicated worker task protected object for each application task, and setting its priority to be identical to that of its application task guarantee that higher priority tasks will always get the computing resource upon demand, even at the expense of blocking possible execution cycles of worker tasks on different domains. We note that the goal in real-time systems is not to use the algorithm that extracts the most available work from the cores, but to use algorithms that can be verified to satisfy the time bounds as well as generate correct calculations. Furthermore, this approach allows not breaking the Ravenscar model in the application tasks single core, whilst allowing accelerating computation in worker cores.

Other systems exist that can take advantage of the simple model presented here (e.g. for runtime simplicity) but that may not have the same strict requirements on static analysis. For those systems we may want to remove some of the assumptions presented in section 5.3, which may lead to a more efficient and balanced utilization of the system resources. This is outside of the scope of this paper, and subject of future research.

Other mappings are clearly possible and supported by the mechanisms that we propose. We have already shown a mapping that dedicates a worker domain for each worker task needing such a resource and one sharing a domain. In particular, where it is known that processor layouts give preference to certain couplings of cores, then these cores can be combined into dispatching domains with work allocation managers defined that optimize such couplings in the configuration portion of the program, and invoked using the straightforward, analyzable methods shown here.

The question naturally arises as to the applicability to other languages. There are real-time operating systems and kernels, as there are other languages and add-ons that permit some level of fine-grained parallelism. The challenge is in pulling them together so that the integration of the combination satisfies the tough requirements of real-time and of converting/dispatching work into multi-core domains. Certainly it is possible, but clearly Ada has a level of integration in the way that it combines real-time tasking with all of the paradigms of a modern programming language necessary to do this today.

6. CONCLUSIONS AND FUTURE WORK

This paper builds on recent work to introduce a model for parallel real-time programming in Ada. We develop and analyze a model where all cores but one are used to provide extra computational power to the application tasks executing in a single core. Because it is rooted in the real-time methodologies prevalent today it leverages those models and techniques to extend the traditional real-time approaches on single core systems to a variety of multi-core possibilities.

In the domain of non-uniform multi-core applications, further exploration of the effects that localized protected object calls have viz-a-viz spin-locks, fair-locks and message-exchanging systems would be useful. On systems where CPU architecture is heterogeneous, the interaction of Ada partitions, shared passive partitions, protected objects and tasklets may permit real-time behaviour across such systems, but further exploration is required.

7. ACKNOWLEDGMENTS

We would like to thank the anonymous reviewers for their valuable comments. This work was partially supported by Portuguese Funds through FCT (Portuguese Foundation for Science and Technology) and by ERDF (European Regional Development Fund) through COMPETE (Operational Programme 'Thematic Factors of Competitiveness'), within VipCore (ref. FCOMP-01-0124-FEDER-015006) project and FCT and the EU ARTEMIS JU funding, within project ref. ARTEMIS/0003/2012, JU grant nr. 333053 (CONCERTO).

8. REFERENCES

[1] H. Ali and L. M. Pinho. A parallel programming model for Ada. In *Proceedings of the 2011 ACM SIGAda International Conference*. ACM, November 2011.

[2] S. K. Baruah, V. Bonifaci, A. Marchetti-Spaccamela, L. Stougie and A. Wiese. A Generalized Parallel Task Model for Recurrent Real-time Processes. In *Proceedings of the 33rd IEEE Real-Time Systems Symposium*, pp. 63-72, 2012.

[3] G. Bosch. Synchronization cannot be implemented as a library. In *Proceedings of the High Integrity Language Technology Conference 2012*, ACM, 2012.

[4] A. Burns and A. Wellings. *Real-Time Systems and Programming Languages: Ada, Real-Time Java and C/Real-Time POSIX*. 4th Edition, Pearson Education Ltd, Edinburg, UK, 2009.

[5] A. Burns and A. Wellings. Locking Policies for Multiprocessor Ada. In *Proceedings 16th International Real-Time Ada Workshop IRTAW 2013*, York, UK, ACM Ada Letters (to be published).

[6] S. Collette, L. Cucu and J. Goossens. Integrating job parallelism in real-time scheduling theory. *Information Processing Letters*, vol. 106, pp. 180–187, May 2008.

[7] R. I. Davis and A. Burns. A survey of hard real-time scheduling for multiprocessor systems. *ACM Computing Survey*, 43(4):35:1–35:44, October 2011.

[8] M. Frigo, C. E. Leiserson and K. H. Randall. The implementation of the Cilk-5 multithreaded language. *SIGPLAN Not.*, 33:212-223, May 1998.

[9] ISO IEC 8652:2012. *Programming Languages and their Environments – Programming Language Ada*. International Standards Organization, Geneva, Switzerland, 2012.

[10] H. Kopetz. *Real-Time Systems: Design Principles for Distributed Embedded Applications*. Springer, 2011.

[11] K. Lakshmanan, S. Kato and R. Rajkumar. Scheduling parallel realtime tasks on multi-core processors. In *Proceedings of the 31st IEEE Real-Time Systems Symposium*, pp. 259 –268, December 2010.

[12] A. Marowka. Parallel computing on any desktop. *Communications of the ACM*. 50:74-78, ACM, September 2007.

[13] S. Michell, B. Moore and L. M. Pinho. Tasklettes – a Fine Grained Parallelism for Ada on Multicores. In *International Conference on Reliable Software Technologies - Ada-Europe 2013*, LNCS 7896, Springer, 2013.

[14] B. Moore. Parallelism generics for Ada 2005 and beyond. In *Proceedings of the ACM SIGAda Annual International Conference*. ACM, 2010.

[15] B. Moore. A comparison of work-sharing, work-seeking, and work-stealing parallelism strategies using Paraffin with Ada 2005. *Ada User Journal*, Volume 32 Number 1, published by Ada Europe, March 2011.

[16] B. Moore, S. Michell and L. M. Pinho. Parallelism in Ada: General Model and Ravenscar. In *Proceedings 16th International Real-Time Ada Workshop IRTAW 2013*, York, UK, ACM Ada Letters (to be published).

[17] A. Saifullah, K. Agrawal, C. Lu and C. Gill. Multi-core real-time scheduling for generalized parallel task models. In *Proceedings of the 32nd IEEE Real-Time Systems Symposium*, Vienna, Austria, December 2011.

APPENDIX – EXAMPLE

This appendix provides an example with the application structured in a one-core system domain and two worker domains. We assume 5 tasks ($P = 5$) all in the application domain. Tasks 3 to 5 read sensors, then update actuators. The devices that manipulate the sensor data and process actuator outputs are assumed to be external to this application. Tasks 1 and 2 perform computations which are amenable to parallelization. These tasks parallelize to worker domains D_1 and D_2 respectively.

A generic interface for a Parallel Manager is provided in the backend. A Parallel Manager implementation may utilize a task pool, and interfaces to sharable task pools are also provided in the backend. The restrictions associated with the Ravenscar Profile, however necessitate a different task pool interface than for the general case. Since task pools only interface with Parallel Managers and not with user code, the backend design allows flexibility in supporting multiple task pool interfaces. This interface contains a set of routines that a pool of Ada tasks call to obtain work to be done, and to return the results of work. A task pool interface which follows the code restrictions of Ravenscar (but not fully the Ravenscar model) is shown here, since it is more relevant to real-time.

```ada
pragma Profile (Ravenscar);

package Ada.Parallel.Ravenscar_Task_Pools is

   -- A Pool_Index uniquely identifies a worker
   -- within the Task Pool
   type Pool_Worker_Count is new
      Worker_Count_Type;

   subtype Pool_Index is Pool_Worker_Count;

   -- A Plan_Index uniquely identifies a worker
   -- within the work plan and Parallel Manager
   type Plan_Worker_Count is new
      Worker_Count_Type;

   subtype Plan_Index is Plan_Worker_Count;

   -- A Work Plan gives the task pool client (the
   -- Parallel Manager) the full control on
   -- how the worker manages and approaches its
   -- work. The task pool only provides
   -- the workers, the work plan defines the work
   -- to be done.

type Work_Plan is limited interface;

procedure Engage (Plan   : in out Work_Plan;
                  Worker : Pool_Index;
                  Item   : Plan_Index)
   is abstract;
-- When a worker starts executing, it engages
-- the work plan. The parallelism manager
-- client decides how to execute the work
-- (tasklets). Engage is called once per
-- tasklet and executes the plan.
-- Upon returning, the Worker is once again
-- idle and returns to the task pool

procedure Starting (Plan      : in out
                                Work_Plan;
                    Requester : Plan_Index;
                    Item      : out Plan_Index)
   is null;
-- Routine that gets called before a work plan
-- is engaged, to allow the plan to initialize
-- any internal state. This routine is meant
-- to be called from within a protected object
-- associated with the pool, and therefore
-- must not be potentially blocking

procedure Completing (Plan : in out Work_Plan;
                      Item : Plan_Index)
   is null;
-- Routine that gets called immediately after
-- the work plan executed the tasklet,
-- to allow the plan to update any internal
-- state. This routine is intended to be
-- called from within a protected object
-- associated with the pool, and therefore
-- must not be potentially blocking.

type Task_Pool_Interface is limited interface;

procedure Reserve (Pool : in out
                          Task_Pool_Interface;
                   Worker_Count :
                          Positive_Worker_Count)
   is abstract
with Pre'Class =>
   Pool.Available_Workers >= Worker_Count;
-- Allows a POP to request and reserve a number
-- of workers from the pool.

procedure Release (Pool : in out
                          Task_Pool_Interface;
                   Worker_Count :
                          Positive_Worker_Count)
   is abstract
with Pre'Class =>
   Pool.Total_Workers - Pool.Available_Workers
   >= Worker_Count;
-- Allows a POP to release the workers it had
-- reserved back to the pool

function Available_Workers (Pool :
                          Task_Pool_Interface)
   return Worker_Count_Type is abstract;
-- Returns the number of workers that may be
-- reserved in the pool.

function Idle_Workers (Pool :
                          Task_Pool_Interface)
   return Worker_Count_Type is abstract;
-- Returns the number of workers that are idle
-- in the pool

function Total_Workers (Pool :
                          Task_Pool_Interface)
   return Positive_Worker_Count is abstract;
-- Returns the total number of workers in the
-- pool

procedure Offer_Work (Pool : in out
                          Task_Pool_Interface;
                      Plan : aliased in out
                          Work_Plan'Class;
                      Item : Plan_Index)
   is abstract
with Pre'Class => Pool.Available_Workers > 0;
-- Allows a Parallel Manager to request a
-- worker from the task pool. The Work plan is
-- offered to the task pool, which is then
-- engaged by an available worker. Note: This
-- routine is intended to be invoked by the
-- parallelism manager, and not exposed to the
-- user client code.
```

```ada
   procedure Offer_Work_To_Group (Pool :
                     in out Task_Pool_Interface;
                              Plan :
                  aliased in out Work_Plan'Class;
                           Worker_Count :
                        Positive_Worker_Count)
      is abstract
   with Pre'Class =>
      Pool.Available_Workers >= Worker_Count;
   -- Allows a Parallel Manager to request a
   -- group of multiple workers from the task
   -- pool. The Work plan is then engaged by each
   -- worker up to the requested Worker_Count.
   -- Note: This routine is intended to be called
   -- by the parallelism manager, and not exposed
   -- to the user client code.

   function Priority (Pool : Task_Pool_Interface)
     return System.Priority is abstract;
   -- Get the priority of the task pool

   procedure Next_Worker_Id (Pool :
                     in out Task_Pool_Interface;
                              Plan :
                  aliased in out Work_Plan'Class;
                           Requester :
                                    Plan_Index;
                           Item :
                              out Plan_Index)
      is null;
   -- Returns the next Plan_Index which will be
   -- uniquely associated with a worker and
   -- corresponding tasklet while it executes the
   -- work plan.

   procedure Finished_Work (Pool    :
                     in out Task_Pool_Interface;
                           Worker : Pool_Index;
                           Plan    :
                  aliased in out Work_Plan'Class;
                           Item    : Plan_Index)
      is null;
   -- Allows a Parallel Manager to indicate to
   -- the task pool that a tasklet has completed
   -- execution. This provides the protected
   -- subprogram context for calling the work plan
   -- Completing primitive to allow the Parallel
   -- Manager to perform any final processing
   -- with synchronization and protection from
   -- other workers.

end Ada.Parallel.Ravenscar_Task_Pools;
```

The specification for a possible implementation of this interface follows.

```ada
pragma Profile (Ravenscar);

with System.Storage_Elements;
with System.Multiprocessors; use System;
with Ada.Parallel.Ravenscar_Task_Pools; use
Ada.Parallel.Ravenscar_Task_Pools;

generic

   Storage_Size :
      System.Storage_Elements.Storage_Count :=
                     Default_Worker_Storage_Size;
   Worker_Priority :
      System.Priority :=
                     System.Default_Priority;
   Number_Of_Workers :
      Pool_Worker_Count := 100;
```

```ada
package Ravenscar_Pool_Implementation is

   type Worker (Core : Multiprocessors.CPU_Range)
      is limited private;

   type Worker_Array is array (1 ..
      Number_Of_Workers) of access Worker;
   -- The Ada tasks in the task pool

   type Task_Pool (Workers : access Worker_Array)
      is limited new Task_Pool_Interface
      with private;
   -- task pool object type that has a pool of
   -- real Ada tasks to process
   -- tasklets that are submitted to the pool for
   -- processing.

private
   ... Implementation Defined
end Ravenscar_Pools_Implementation;
```

The Application specification identifies and configures the application tasks and associated task pools.

```ada
private with Ravenscar_Pools_Implementation;

package The_Ravens_Car_Application is

   -- We assume here that Sensors and Actuators
   -- are maintained by external devices. Sensors
   -- can be read by the Ada application, and
   -- actuators can be set by the Ada
   -- application.

   type External_Device is new Float with Atomic;

   subtype Sensor_Type   is External_Device;
   subtype Actuator_Type is External_Device;

   type External_Data_Buffer
      is array (Integer range <>) of Integer
      with Atomic_Components;

   Camera_Data :
      External_Data_Buffer  (1 .. 1_000_000) :=
                              (others => 0);
   -- Video capture

   Brakes : Actuator_Type;
   -- Controls the brakes of the vehicle

   Audio_Data :
      External_Data_Buffer (1 .. 2**20) :=
                              (others => 0);
   Voice_Command : Actuator_Type;
   -- Indicates current voice command to process

   Desired_Temperature : Sensor_Type;
   -- Monitors Desired temperature
   Thermostat : Actuator_Type;
   -- Controls the thermostat

   Desired_Direction : Sensor_Type;
   -- Monitors GPS direction
   Steering_Wheel : Actuator_Type;
   -- Controls direction of vehicle

   Desired_Velocity : Sensor_Type;
   -- Monitors the desired velocity

   Speed : Actuator_Type;
   -- Controls the speed
```

```ada
    private
        -- Tasks T1 and T2 get the Camera and Audio
        -- data and calculate the actuator
        -- output. We assume that this can be
        -- parallelized.  Create the application tasks

        task AT1 with Priority => 1, CPU => 1;
        -- Controls vehicles brakes via camera input

        task AT2 with Priority => 2, CPU => 1;
        -- Interprets voice data commands

        task AT3 with Priority => 3, CPU => 1;
        -- Controls vehicle direction via GPS input

        task AT4 with Priority => 4, CPU => 1;
        -- Controls vehicle speed

        task AT5 with Priority => 5, CPU => 1;
        -- Controls air temperature


        -- Create the task pools
        package D1_Task_Pool is new
            Ravenscar_Pools_Implementation
                (Storage_Size        =>
            Parallel.Default_Worker_Storage_Size,
                Worker_Priority    => 1,
                Number_Of_Workers => 4);

        Worker1 :
            aliased D1_Task_Pool.Worker (Core => 2);
        Worker2 :
            aliased D1_Task_Pool.Worker (Core => 3);
        Worker3 :
            aliased D1_Task_Pool.Worker (Core => 4);
        Worker4 :
            aliased D1_Task_Pool.Worker (Core => 5);

        D1_Workers :
            aliased D1_Task_Pool.Worker_Array :=
            (1 => Worker1'Access,
             2 => Worker2'Access,
             3 => Worker3'Access,
             4 => Worker4'Access);

        TP1 : aliased D1_Task_Pool.Task_Pool (
                Workers => D1_Workers'Access);
        -- Task Pool for AT1

        package D2_Task_Pool is new
            Ravenscar_Pools_Implementation
                (Storage_Size        =>
            Parallel.Default_Worker_Storage_Size,
                Worker_Priority    => 2,
                Number_Of_Workers => 2);

        Worker5 :
            aliased D2_Task_Pool.Worker (Core => 6);
        Worker6 :
            aliased D2_Task_Pool.Worker (Core => 7);

        D2_Workers :
            aliased D2_Task_Pool.Worker_Array :=
            (1 => Worker5'Access,
             2 => Worker6'Access);

        TP2 : aliased D2_Task_Pool.Task_Pool (
                Workers => D2_Workers'Access);
        -- Task pool for AT2

end The_Ravens_Car_Application;

-- Change Cores of Worker 5-6 to overlap cores of
-- Worker 1-4  to change to Mapping 2
-- Note that to switch to MAPPING 2, nothing
-- needs to be done in the tasks AT(1 or 2) or WT
```

The actual code of the applications can be based on existent sequential code, with only adding parallelization information in the loops in tasks T_1 and T_2. For completeness we show the code.

```ada
with Ada.Real_Time; use Ada;
with Parallel.Functional_Reducing_Loops.
                    Ravenscar_Work_Seeking;
with Parallel.Functional_Reducing_Recursion_
                    Ravenscar_Work_Sharing;
with Parallel.One_Shot_Wait_Free_
                    Synchronous_Barriers;
use Parallel.One_Shot_Wait_Free_
                    Synchronous_Barriers;

package body The_Ravens_Car_Application is

    Start_Time :
        constant Real_Time.Time := Real_Time.Clock;
    use type Real_Time.Time;

    task body AT1
        -- Suppose AT1 controls the brakes of the
        -- vehicle by monitoring camera views of
        -- the road
    is
        package Integer_Loops is
            new Parallel.Functional_Reducing_Loops
            (Result_Type => Integer,
             Reducer => Integer'Max,
             Identity_Value => Integer'First,
             Iteration_Index_Type => Integer);

        package Max_Loop is new
            Integer_Loops.Ravenscar_Work_Seeking;

        Max_Value : Integer := Integer'First;

        Next_Execution :
            Real_Time.Time := Start_Time;
        Period :
            constant Real_Time.Time_Span :=
                        Real_Time.Milliseconds (1);

    begin  -- AT1 body
        loop
            delay until Next_Execution;

            for I in Camera_Data'Range
                with Parallel,
                    Task_Pool => TP1,
                    Accumulator => Max_Value,
                    Parallel_Manager =>
                        Max_Loop.Work_Seeking_Manager
            loop
                Max := Integer'Max (
                            Max, Camera_Data (I));
            end loop;

            -- Assume that the brake value is the
            -- maximum value found in the camera
            -- data. (Not at all realistic, a
            -- realistic computation would be too
            -- complex to show here)
            Brakes := Actuator_Type (Max_Value);
            Next_Execution := Next_Execution +Period;
        end loop;
    end AT1;

--------------------------------------------------
    task body AT2
    is
        -- Suppose AT2 processes voice command
        -- audio data, and acts on the interpreted
        -- commands
```

```ada
   --  The processing shown here is not
   --  realistic, but nevertheless shows
   --  parallel processing in two phases.

   --  The simplistic algorithm shown here
   --  calculates the average of the  array
   --  segment, then adds 1 to all values
   --  above the average, and then substracts
   --  1 from all values below the average.

   --  eg: An array of 8 elements with values
   --  from 1 .. 8
   --  there are only two worker tasks in the
   --  task pool, therefore we indicate a
   --  chunk_Size of 4 and the compiler  will
   --  divide the work in two

   --  data: 1,  2,  3,  4,  5,  6,  7,  8
   --
   --  pass 1 (two workers in parallel):
   --            ------------  -------------
   --    Sum:         10,            26
   --    Reduced Sum:        36

   --  Average calculated by AT2: 4.5

   --  pass 2 (two workers in parallel):
   --            ------------  -------------
   --  data: 0,  1,  2,  3,  6,  7,  8,  9

   package Integer_Loops is
      new Parallel.Functional_Reducing_Loops
        (Result_Type => Integer,
         Reducer => "+",
         Identity_Value => 0,
         Iteration_Index_Type => Integer);

   package Avg_Loop is new
        Integer_Loops.Ravenscar_Work_Sharing;

   Sum_Value : Integer := 0;
   Avg_Value : Float;


   Next_Execution   :
        Real_Time.Time := Start_Time;
   Period           :
        constant Real_Time.Time_Span :=
                 Real_Time.Milliseconds (5);


begin  --  AT2 body

   loop
      delay until Next_Execution;

      for I in 1 .. 8
         with Parallel,
              Task_Pool => TP2,
              Accumulator => Sum_Value,
              Parallel_Manager =>
                Avg_Loop.Work_Sharing_Manager,
              Chunk_Size => 4
      loop
         Sum_Value := Audio_Data(I) +Sum_Value;
      end loop;
      --  Parallel first phase calculating
      --  aggregated sum

      Avg_Value := Float(Sum_Value) / 8.0;
      --  Sequential phase calculating the
      --  average
```

```ada
      for I in 1 .. 8
         with Parallel,
              Task_Pool => TP2,
              Chunk_Size => 4
      loop
         if (Float(Audio_Data(I)) >
                              Avg_Value) then
            Audio_Data(I) := Audio_Data(I) + 1;
         elsif (Float(Audio_Data(I)) <
                              Avg_Value) then
            Audio_Data(I) := Audio_Data(I) - 1;
         end if;
      end loop;
      --  Parallel second phase updating values

      Next_Execution := Next_Execution +Period;
   end loop;
end AT2;

-----------------------------------------------------
   task body AT3 is
      --  Suppose AT3 maintains the direction of
      --  the vehicle according to
      --  current route instructions from a
      --  GPS device
      Next_Execution :
         Real_Time.Time := Start_Time;
      Period :
         constant Real_Time.Time_Span :=
                  Real_Time.Milliseconds (10);
   begin
      loop
         delay until Next_Execution;
         Steering_Wheel := Desired_Direction;
         Next_Execution := Next_Execution +Period;
      end loop;
   end AT3;

-----------------------------------------------------
   task body AT4 is
      --  Suppose AT4 maintains the
      --  cruise control speed
      Next_Execution :
         Real_Time.Time := Start_Time;
      Period :
         constant Real_Time.Time_Span :=
                  Real_Time.Milliseconds (100);
   begin
      loop
         delay until Next_Execution;
         Speed := Desired_Velocity;
         Next_Execution := Next_Execution +Period;
      end loop;
   end AT4;

-----------------------------------------------------
   task body AT5 is
      --  Suppose AT5 maintains the cabin
      --  temperature by controlling heating/AC
      Next_Execution :
         Real_Time.Time := Start_Time;
      Period :
         constant Real_Time.Time_Span :=
                  Real_Time.Minutes (1);
   begin
      loop
         delay until Next_Execution;
         Thermostat := Desired_Temperature;
         Next_Execution := Next_Execution +Period;
      end loop;
   end AT5;

end The_Ravens_Car_Application;
```

Bringing Safe, Dynamic Parallel Programming to the SPARK Verifiable Subset of Ada

S. Tucker Taft
AdaCore
24 Muzzey Street, 3rd Floor
Lexington, MA 02421 USA
+1-781-750-8068 x220
taft@adacore.com

ABSTRACT

SPARK is a verifiable subset of Ada which has been in use for over 20 years for developing the most critical parts of complex real-time applications [1][2]. A restricted subset of the Ada tasking model is included in the newer versions of SPARK ("RavenSPARK"), but this is a very static model, with a fixed number of tasks and minimal task interaction [3]. In this presentation we will describe an extension of SPARK to support safe highly parallel programming, targeted at the growing number of multicore and manycore processors appearing on the market today.

Categories and Subject Descriptors

D.1.3 [**Programming Techniques**]: Concurrent Programming – parallel programming; D.2.4 [Software Engineering]: Software/Program Verification – formal methods, reliability; [**Programming Languages**]: Language Constructs and Features – concurrent programming structures, dynamic storage management, recursion.

General Terms

Algorithms, Reliability, Languages, Verification.

Keywords

Multicore programming, parallel programming, pointer-free programming, SPARK, Ada.

1. PARALLEL SPARK

SPARK is a verifiable subset of *Ada* which has been in use for over 20 years for developing the most critical parts of complex real-time applications {1}[2]. A restricted subset of the Ada tasking model is included in the newer versions of SPARK (*RavenSPARK*), but this is a very static model, with a fixed number of tasks and minimal task interaction [3]. In this presentation we will describe an extension of SPARK to support safe highly parallel programming, targeted at the growing number of multicore and manycore processors appearing on the market today.

HILT'13, November 10–14 2013, Pittsburgh, PA, USA
Copyright is held by the owner/author(s). Publication rights licensed to ACM.
ACM 978-1-4503-2466-3/13/11…$15.00.
http://dx.doi.org/10.1145/2527269.2527279

This parallel version of SPARK, which we will call *Sparkel* in this presentation, preserves the verifiable orientation of SPARK, while relaxing the static approach to tasking and storage management. Sparkel adopts a model where all expressions have implicitly parallel semantics, that is, given an expression such as "F(X) + G(Y)," the rules of Sparkel ensure that it is always safe to evaluate F(X) and G(Y) in parallel and then combine their results. That is, Sparkel provides safe parallelism *by construction*.

Sparkel also extends the SPARK storage model while preserving its pointer-free, alias-free approach, by allowing objects to grow and shrink dynamically. The basic extension is that every type T is augmented with one extra value, called **null**, but only objects or components declared with "Obj : **optional** T" may store this extra value. Objects declared simply "Obj : T" are not permitted to have a null value. Types may be *recursive*, so long as at least one component in the recursion is declared **optional**. Hence, a binary tree may be declared simply as:

```
type Binary_Tree is record
    Payload : Data_Type;
    Left : optional Binary_Tree;
    Right : optional Binary_Tree;
end record;
```

A Binary_Tree object will grow if its Left or Right subtree goes from a null to a non-null value, and will shrink if a non-null subtree is set to null. Hence, Sparkel supports recursive, dynamic data structures while preserving the pointer-free, alias-free semantic model. Note that Left and Right are objects with *value* semantics, not pointers, and do not share storage with any other object.

By remaining pointer free, these kinds of dynamic objects directly support the *divide-and-conquer* approach to safe parallel computation, where separate threads of control may concurrently process the Left and Right subtree of such an object, knowing that they will never "run into" each other because there is no sharing of data between distinct (sub) objects.

In addition to the implicit parallel semantics of expression evaluation, Sparkel permits explicit parallelism to be expressed using "||" instead of ";" to separate statements that may be performed in parallel, as well as loops explicitly marked as **parallel** rather than **reverse** or **forward**, By default, the Sparkel compiler will try to execute statements and loops in parallel even without these explicit notations, provided there are no data dependences. By contrast, when parallel execution is explicitly requested, it is a compile-time error if there are any data dependences.

In this presentation we will illustrate how Sparkel relates to SPARK and Ada as well as other languages specifically designed to support multicore programming. We will show how the parallel and extensible object features of Sparkel enable inherently safe, highly productive parallel programming

2. A LONGER EXAMPLE

As a longer example of what a Sparkel program looks like, here we illustrate a program that solves the N-Queens [6] problem. Some syntax differences to note relative to SPARK and Ada include the use of **func** and **proc** as shorthands for **function** and **procedure**, several new forms of **loop**s, direct instantiation of types rather than requiring an intermediate instantiation of an enclosing package, with generic actuals inside <> rather than (). Similarly, [] are used rather than () for indexing. The operator "|" is used for generalized concatenation/combination. Annotations are in {}, though support for Ada 2012's **with Pre => ...** syntax is forthcoming. See further documentation at [4].

```
generic
   Max_N : Univ_Integer := 8;
package N_Queens is
   -- Place N queens on an NxN checkerboard so that none of them can
   -- "take" each other.

   type Chess_Unit is new Integer< -Max_N*2 .. Max_N*2 >;
      -- An integer big enough to represent values -Max_N*2 .. +Max_N*2

   subtype Row is Chess_Unit; -- A subrange in 1..Max_N
   subtype Column is Chess_Unit; -- A subrange
   type Solution is new Array<optional Column, Row>;
      -- A "solution" is an array of Column's, indexed by "Row."
      -- It indicates in which Column a queen of the given Row is located
      -- An example solution would be:  2 8 6 1 3 5 7 4
      --   meaning that the queen in row 1 is at column 2,
      --   the queen in row 2 is at column 8, the queen in
      --   row 3 is at column 6, and so on.

   func Place_Queens(N : Row := Max_N) return Vector<Solution>
      {for all Sol of Place_Queens => for all Col of Sol => Col not null};
      -- Produce a vector of solutions, with the requirement
      -- that for each solution, there are non-null column numbers
      -- specified for each row of the checkerboard.
end package N_Queens;

package body N_Queens is
   subtype Sum_Range is Chess_Unit; -- in 2..2*Max_N;
      -- Sum_Range is used for diagonals where the row+column is the
      -- same throughout the diagonal.
   subtype Diff_Range is Chess_Unit; -- in (1-Max_N) .. (Max_N-1);
      -- Diff_Range is used for diagonals where row-column is the
      -- same throughout the diagonal.
   type Sum is new Countable_Set<Sum_Range>;
      -- This type of set keeps track of which Sum_Range diagonals
      -- have a queen on them already.
   type Diff is new Countable_Set<Diff_Range>;
      -- This type of set keeps track of which Diff_Range diagonals
      -- have a queen on them already.

   type Solution_State is record
      C : Column;    -- Current column
      Trial : Solution; -- Trial solution, some col#s still null
      Diag_Sum : Sum;  -- Set of "sum" diagonals in use
      Diag_Diff : Diff; -- Set of "diff" diagnoals in use
   end record;

   -- We build up a solution state progressively as we move
   -- across the checkerboard, one column at a time.
   func Initial_State(N : Row) return Solution_State is
      return (C => 1, Trial => Create(1..N, null),
        Diag_Sum => [], Diag_Diff => []);
```

```
   end func Initial_State;

   func Is_Acceptable(S : Solution_State; R : Row) return Boolean is
      -- Is_Acceptable returns True if the next queen could be
      -- placed in row R.
      return S.Trial[R] is null and then
        (R+S.C) not in S.Diag_Sum and then
        (R-S.C) not in S.Diag_Diff;
   end func Is_Acceptable;

   func Current_Column(S : Solution_State) return Column is
      -- Current_Column indicates which column we are working on.
      return S.C;
   end func Current_Column;

   func Next_State(S : Solution_State; R : Row) return Solution_State is
      -- Next_State returns a Solution_State produced by
      -- adding a queen at (Current_Column(S), R).
      return (C => S.C+1,
        Trial    => S.Trial | [R => S.C],
        Diag_Sum => S.Diag_Sum | (R+S.C),
        Diag_Diff => S.Diag_Diff | (R-S.C));
   end func Next_State;

   func Final_Result(S : Solution_State; R : Row) return Solution is
      -- Final_Result returns a result produced by adding a queen
      -- at (Columns.Last, R) to a solution with all other columns
      -- placed.
      return S.Trial | [R => S.C];
   end func Final_Result;

   func Partial_Solution(S : Solution_State) return Solution is
      -- Return partial solution thus far
      return S.Trial;
   end func Partial_Solution;

exports

   func Place_Queens(N : Row := Max_N) return Vector<Solution>
      {for all Sol of Place_Queens => for all Col of Sol => Col not null}
      -- Produce a vector of solutions, with the requirement
      -- that for each solution, there are non-null column numbers
      -- specified for each row of the checkerboard.
   is
      const Rows : Countable_Range<Chess_Unit> := 1..N;
      var Solutions : protected Vector<Solution> := [];

      Outer_Loop:
      for State : Solution_State := Initial_State(N) loop
         -- Iterate over the columns

         for R in Rows parallel loop
            -- Iterate over the rows
            if Is_Acceptable(State, R) then
               -- Found a Row/Column combination not on any diagonal
               -- already occupied.
               if Current_Column(State) < N then
                  -- Keep going since haven't reached Nth column.
                  const Next := Next_State(State, R);
                  continue loop Outer_Loop with State => Next;
               else
                  -- All done, remember trial result with last queen placed
                  const Final := Final_Result(State, R);
                  Solutions |= Final;
               end if;
            end if;
         end loop;
      end loop Outer_Loop;
      return Solutions;

   end func Place_Queens;
end package N_Queens;
```

```
proc Test_N_Queens(N : Univ_Integer) is

  package Max_12_Queens is new N_Queens<Max_N => 12>;

  var Results := Max_12_Queens.Place_Queens(N);
  Println("Number of results with " | N | " queens = " | |Results|);

  for each [I => Result] of Results forward loop
    Print("Result #" | I);
    for each Col of Result forward loop
      Print(" " | Col);
    end loop;
    Print('\n');
  end loop;

end proc Test_N_Queens;
```

3. ACKNOWLEDGMENTS

The designs of Sparkel and the ParaSail language [5] which preceded it were heavily influenced by the anti-aliasing rules and other verifiability-oriented rules of the SPARK subset of Ada.

4. REFERENCES

[1] Chapman, R., *Industrial experience with SPARK*, Ada Letters. XX(4), 64–68 (2000).

[2] O'Neill, I. et al, *The Formal Semantics of SPARK83*, Program Validation Limited 1994.

[3] SPARK Team, *SPARK Examiner, The SPARK Ravenscar Profile*, Praxis, 2008, available at: http://intelligent-systems.altran.com/fileadmin/medias/0.commons/documents/Technology_documents/examiner_ravenscar.pdf (retrieved 8/2013)..

[4] *Sparkel* web site, http://www.sparkel.org .

[5] Taft, S. Tucker, *ParaSail: Less is More with Multicore*, www.embedded.com, 2012, available at http://www.embedded.com/design/other/4375616/ParaSail--Less-is-more-with-multicore (retrieved 9/23/2013).

[6] Wirth, Niklaus, *Algorithms + Data Structures = Programs*, Prentice-Hall, ISBN 0-13-022418-9, 1976.

Up and Out: Scaling Formal Analysis Using Model-Based Development and Architecture Modeling*

Michael W. Whalen
Department of Computer Science and Engineering
University of Minnesota
200 Union Street, Minneapolis, Minnesota 55455
whalen@cs.umn.edu

ABSTRACT

Systems are naturally constructed in hierarchies in which design choices made at higher levels of abstraction "flow down" to requirements on system components at lower levels of abstraction. Thus, whether an aspect of the system is a design choice or a requirement depends largely on oneâĂŹs vantage point within the hierarchy of system components. Furthermore, systems are often constructed middle-out rather than top-down; compatibility with existing systems and architectures, or availability of specific components influences high-level requirements. We believe that requirements and architectural design should be more closely aligned: that requirements models must account for hierarchical system construction, and that architectural design notations must better support specification of requirements for system components.

In this presentation, I describe tools supporting iterative development of architecture and verification based on software models. We represent the hierarchical composition of the system in the Architecture Analysis & Design Language (AADL), and use an extension to the AADL language to describe requirements at different levels of abstraction for compositional verification. To describe and verify component-level behavior, we use Simulink and Stateflow and multiple analysis tools.

Categories and Subject Descriptors

D.2.1 [**Software Engineering**]: Requirements/Specifications—*Methodologies - Requirements flow down*; D.2.4 [**Software Engineering**]: Software/Program Verification—*Formal methods; Model checking*

Keywords

Compositional Verification; System Decomposition; Cyber Physical Systems

*This work has been partially supported by NSF grants CNS-0931931 and CNS-1035715.

HILT'13, November 12–14, 2013, Pittsburgh, PA, USA.
ACM 978-1-4503-2467-0/13/11.
http://dx.doi.org/10.1145/2527269.2527293 .

1. CONTENTS

Software is ubiquitous in safety-critical systems, which have the potential to cause loss of life, injury, or other serious damage to property and environment. The size and complexity of this software continues to grow, making it ever more difficult to capture the correct requirements, design the software correctly, and verify to a high level of confidence that we have the right requirements and that the software indeed satisfies those requirements. In order to field next-generation safety-critical systems with confidence, it will be necessary to augment manual testing with a variety of automated analyses.

The University of Minnesota Software Engineering Center and Rockwell Collins Advanced Technology Center have jointly been researching formal verification, metrics and automation strategies for testing, and requirements capture for more than 15 years. The goals are to improve system requirements, reduce verification and validation (V&V) costs while increasing rigor. In previous work, we constructed a translator framework that allows us to automatically translate from some of the most popular commercial model-based development languages (MATLAB Simulink/Stateflow [4] and SCADE [3] into a variety of model checkers and theorem provers. This framework was used to rigorously analyze several industrial applications written in Simulink [6]. In addition, this framework was used to study automated test generation and the effectiveness of automated test generation for a variety of metrics [7, 2].

While we have become better at demonstrating that leaf-level components meet their requirements, checking whether component-level requirements are sufficient to demonstrate the satisfaction of higher-level requirements is still an area of ongoing research. Not surprisingly, component integration has become the most important source of errors in systems. In fact, while techniques for specifying and verifying individual components have become highly automated, the most common tools used to specify the complex system architectures in which they are embedded remain word processors, spreadsheets, and drawing packages. Better support for decomposition of requirements throughout the system architecture, and subsequent verification that these decompositions are sound, is of paramount importance.

To this end, we have been creating an open-source compositional reasoning system on top of AADL called AGREE [1]. Assume-guarantee contracts [5] are used for capturing the information needed to reason about system-level properties. In this formulation, guarantees correspond to the component requirements. These guarantees are verified separately as part of the component development process, either by formal or traditional means. Assumptions correspond to the environmental constraints that were used in verifying the component requirements. For formally verified components, they are the assertions or invariants on the component inputs that were used in the proof process. A contract specifies precisely the information that is needed to reason about the componentâĂŹs interaction with other parts of the system. Furthermore, contract mechanism supports a hierarchical decomposition of verification process that follows the natural hierarchy in the system model.

In this talk, I describe work applying both component-level and compositional verification and steps towards technology transfer of verification tools.

2. ACKNOWLEDGEMENTS

I would like to thank Mats Heimdahl and Sanjai Rayadurgam at UMN and Andrew Gacek and Darren Cofer at Rockwell Collins for their insight and assistance in structuring and debugging the architectural models, and for developing JKind and AGREE.

3. REFERENCES

[1] D. D. Cofer, A. Gacek, S. P. Miller, M. W. Whalen, B. LaValley, and L. Sha. Compositional verification of architectural models. In A. E. Goodloe and S. Person, editors, *Proceedings of the 4th NASA Formal Methods Symposium (NFM 2012)*, volume 7226, pages 126–140, Berlin, Heidelberg, April 2012. Springer-Verlag.

[2] G. Devaraj, M. Heimdahl, and D. Liang. Coverage-directed test generation with model checkers: Challenges and opportunities. *Computer Software and Applications Conference, Annual International*, 1:455–462, 2005.

[3] Esterel-Technologies. SCADE Suite product description. http://www.esterel-technologies.com/v2/scadeSuiteForSafetyCriticalSoftwareDevelopment/index.html, 2004.

[4] Mathworks Inc. Simulink product web site. http://www.mathworks.com/products/simulink.

[5] K. L. McMillan. Circular compositional reasoning about liveness. Technical Report 1999-02, Cadence Berkeley Labs, Berkeley, CA 94704, 1999.

[6] S. P. Miller, M. W. Whalen, and D. D. Cofer. Software model checking takes off. *Commun. ACM*, 53(2):58–64, 2010.

[7] A. Rajan, M. Whalen, and M. Heimdahl. The Effect of Program and Model Structure on MC/DC Test Adequacy Coverage. In *Proceedings of 30th International Conference on Software Engineering (ICSE)*, 2008. Available at http://crisys.cs.umn.edu/ICSE08.pdf.

4. SHORT BIO:

Dr. Michael Whalen is the Program Director at the University of Minnesota Software Engineering Center. He has 15 years experience in software development and analysis, including 10 years experience in Model-Based Development and safety-critical systems. Dr. Whalen has developed simulation, translation, testing, and formal analysis tools for Model-Based Development languages including Simulink, Stateflow, Lustre, and RSML-e. He has led successful formal verification projects on large industrial avionics models, including displays (Rockwell-Collins ADGS-2100 Window Manager), redundancy management and control allocation (AFRL CerTA FCS program) and autoland (AFRL CerTA CPD program). Dr. Whalen was the lead developer of the Rockwell-Collins Gryphon tool suite, which can be used for compilation, test-case generation, and formal analysis of Simulink/Stateflow models. This tool suite has been used both for academic research and industrial verification projects. He is currently working on tools for architectural analysis in AADL.

Dr. Whalen is a frequent speaker and author on the use of formal methods and automated testing, with several invited presentations, six journal publications, one book chapter, over 35 conference and workshop papers, and 10 contractor and technical reports published. His PhD dissertation involved using higher-order abstract syntax as a basis for a provably-correct code generation tool from the RSML-e specification language into a subset of C. His interests include novel uses of model checking, test generation, theorem proving, and random search simulation tools to reduce the cost and manual effort required for systems and software validation for critical systems.

An Approach to Integration of Complex Systems: the SAVI Virtual Integration Process

Donald T. Ward
Aerospace Vehicle Systems Institute
3126 TAMU – TSHB #127
College Station, TX 77843-3126
+1-979-862-2316
SAVIPgm@gmail.com

David A. Redman
Aerospace Vehicle Systems Institute
3126 TAMU – TSHB #127
College Station, TX 77843-3126
+1-979-862-2316
dredman@tamu.edu

Bruce A. Lewis
United States Army
AMRDEC/SED
Redstone Arsenal, AL 35898
+1-256-698-0164
bruce.a.lewis.civ@mail.mil

ABSTRACT

The SAVI approach to integration embodies three fundamental concepts: (1) an architecture-centric emphasis (wrapped around an annotated architectural model with analyses carried out at the system level after modifications); (2) a component-based decomposition of elements of the system that support a building block approach; and (3) a unique level of consistency checking to assure compatibility for the physical and logical integration through analyses using the annotated architectural model. This level of consistency checking allows a "single truth" across the multi-domain model set. Thus, this unique architectural model implements the SAVI mantra of "integrate, analyze – then build" to address a range of virtual integration issues. Careful safeguards to protect the integrity of intellectual property for each member of the development team are provided through the SAVI Model Repository and Data Exchange Layer (SMR/DEL). These two core information-sharing elements of the VIP will eventually depend heavily on standards-based (likely ISO 10303-239) information exchange and the SAVI team has taken steps recently to cooperate with global collaborators, both in the United States and in Europe in this type of information exchange. This sort of standards-based data exchange also offers considerable promise for protection of sensitive information within a system development with competing suppliers.

The paper describes how multiple architectural definition languages (specifically SysML and AADL) have been utilized in developing the core of this model-based analysis approach. The objective is to exploit strengths of both these languages while maintaining capability to translate between both variations of architectural models. The primary means of accomplishing this two-way translation is an extension of the translator generated by Cofer, et al, for the DARPA META program. This translator currently operates bidirectionally between SysML and AADL but only upon a rather limited subset of SysML capabilities but the SAVI team expects to see this two-way capability broadened with each incremental development phase of the VIP. Extensive use of recent new annexes for AADL, notably the Error Model Annex, has been a means of automating system safety analysis tools (like Functional Hazard Assessments, Failure Modes and

Effects Analyses, and Fault Tree Analyses) that underpin broader System Safety Analysis.

Another characteristic embedded in the SAVI VIP is a comprehensive form of consistency checking designed to evaluate integration of components and alterations of such components. At least six types of consistency are considered in a SAVI-compliant integration effort: (1) interface consistency, (2) compositional consistency, (3) constraint consistency, (4) behavioral consistency, (5) version consistency, and (6) verification consistency. Moreover, whenever a modification is made to any component, not only are these elements of consistency to be addressed, the effect of the modification on the entire system must be quantitatively analyzed using the SAVI annotated architectural model for the modified system. Each system considered under the SAVI paradigm is analyzed for system properties required to meet its performance specification using this architectural approach. The AADL portion of the architectural model structure allows quantitative evaluation of the system impact of each change made to the substructure. In this sense, the SAVI approach facilitates quantitative trade studies aimed at system behavior during each iteration in the design loop.

Categories and Subject Descriptors

B.3.3 [**Performance Analysis and Design Aids**]: *Formal models, Simulation, Worst-case analysis*
C.0 [**COMPUTER SYSTEMS ARCHITECTURE: GENERAL**]: *Hardware/software interface, System architecture, Systems specification methodology*
C.3 [**SPECIAL-PURPOSE AND APPLICATION-BASED SYSTEMS**]: *Real-time and embedded systems*
C.4 [**PERFORMANCE OF SYSTEMS**]: *Design studies, Fault tolerance, Modeling techniques, Performance attributes*
D.2.9 [**Management**]: *Software configuration management, Software process models*
D.2.11 [**Software Architectures**]: *Data abstraction, Languages(architectural, description, interconnection, definition),*
D.2.12 [**Interoperability**]: *Data mapping, Distributed objects, Interface definition languages*
D.2.13 [**Reusable Software**]: *Reusable libraries, Reuse model*
H.2.5 [**Heterogeneous Databases**]: *Data translation*
I.6 [**SIMULATION AND MODELING**]: *All major category descriptors*

General Terms

Algorithms, Management, Measurement, Documentation, Performance, Design, Economics, Reliability, Security, Human Factors, Standardization, Languages, Verification.

ACM acknowledges that this contribution was authored or co-authored by an employee, contractor or affiliate of the United States government. As such, the Government retains a nonexclusive, royalty-free right to publish or reproduce this article, or to allow others to do so, for Government purposes only.
HILT 2013, November 10-14, 2013, Pittsburgh, PA, USA
Copyright is held by the owner/author(s). Publication rights licensed to ACM.
ACM 978-1-4503-2466-3/13/11...$15.00.
http://dx.doi.org/10.1145/2527269.2527275

Keywords
Annotated architectural model, SAVI model repository, SAVI Data Exchange Layer, Consistency Checking.

1. INTRODUCTION

Several industrial concerns, along with the FAA, DoD, and NASA, have been cooperating over approximately the past seven years to exploit the promise of model-based systems engineering by concentrating on the integration process of aircraft development as the key systems engineering process for attacking exponential growth in complexity for this class of systems. Three phases of Proof of Concept have been completed and this paper documents specifically the results for the first phase of "productionizing" the Virtual Integration Process (VIP). The primary focus in this latest stage of development is wrapped around safety analyses associated with a major subsystem for an aircraft (the wheel braking system or WBS) as suggested by SAE ARP 6110 [1] and associated system safety guidelines.

2. SAVI CORE PRINCIPLES

The SAVI approach to integration embodies three fundamental concepts: (1) an architecture-centric emphasis (wrapped around an annotated architectural model with analyses carried out at the system level after modifications); (2) a component-based decomposition of elements of the system that support a building block approach; and (3) a unique level of consistency checking to assure compatibility for the physical and logical integration through analyses using the annotated architectural model. This level of consistency checking allows a "single truth" across the multi-domain model set. Thus, this unique architectural model implements the SAVI mantra of "integrate, analyze – then build" to address a range of virtual integration issues. Careful safeguards to protect the integrity of intellectual property for each member of the development team are provided through the SAVI Model Repository and Data Exchange Layer (SMR/DEL). These two core information-sharing elements of the VIP will eventually depend heavily on standards-based (likely ISO 10303-239) information exchange and the SAVI team has taken steps recently to cooperate with global collaborators, both in the United States and in Europe in this type of information exchange. This sort of standards-based data exchange also offers considerable promise for protection of sensitive information within a system development with competing suppliers.

Another of the core principles that SAVI pursues is to avoid dependence on any single source element; SAVI carefully evaluates all elements of the SAVI tool chain to ensure that the VIP is not locked into a single source at any stage. Just as the standards mentioned above are not bound to a single source of support, the SAVI model-based integration process must remain "tool-neutral".

3. SAVI CURRENT STATUS
3.1 Multiple Architectural Languages

Multiple architectural definition languages (specifically SysML and AADL) have been utilized in developing the core of this model-based analysis approach. The objective is to exploit strengths of both these languages while maintaining capability to translate between both variations of architectural models. The primary means of accomplishing this two-way translation is an extension of the translator developed by Cofer and his co-workers [2] for the DARPA META program. This translator currently operates in a two-way sense (between SysML and AADL) only upon a rather limited subset of SysML capabilities but the SAVI team expects to see this two-way capability broadened with each incremental development phase of the VIP. Extensive use of recent new annexes for AADL, notably the Error Model Annex, has been a means of automating system safety analysis tools (like Functional Hazard Assessments, Failure Modes and Effects Analyses, and Fault Tree Analyses) that underpin broader System Safety Analysis.

3.2 SAVI Consistency Checking

Another characteristic embedded in the SAVI VIP is a comprehensive form of consistency checking designed to evaluate integration of components and alterations of such components. At least six types of consistency are considered in a SAVI-compliant integration effort: (1) interface consistency, (2) compositional consistency, (3) constraint consistency, (4) behavioral consistency, (5) version consistency, and (6) verification consistency. Moreover, whenever a modification is made to any component, not only are these elements of consistency to be addressed, the effect of the modification on the entire system is quantitatively analyzed using the SAVI annotated architectural model for the modified system. Each system considered under the SAVI paradigm is examined for system properties required to meet its performance specification using this architectural approach. The AADL portion of the architectural model structure allows this quantitative evaluation of the system impact for each change made to the substructure. In this sense, the SAVI approach facilitates quantitative trade studies aimed at the system behavior during each iteration in the design loop.

3.3 SAVI Version 1.0 Capabilities

Finally, the paper presents excerpts from recent demonstrations prepared for internal reviews of VIP and SMR/DEL specifications within each participating company of the SAVI team. These demonstrations highlight how the SAVI VIP promotes trade studies, supports consistency checking, speeds up integration during System Safety Analysis, and helps assure that physical and logical integration proceeds smoothly by minimizing the amount of rework necessary after the integration process is completed. Table 1 summarizes the current capabilities of the SAVI Virtual Integration Process.

Table 1. Current Capabilities of VIP Version 1.0

- *Capability to model and analyze WBSS subsystems and components in AADL*
  - ❖ *Analysis includes Functional Hazard Assessment, Fault-tree analysis, and Markov-Chain analysis (what about FMECA, Julien?) and ultimately a Preliminary System Safety Analysis (PSSA)*
  - ❖ *Schedulability for all computational components*
  - ❖ *CPU load analysis within system elements*
- *Capability to translate both ways between SysML and AADL for system model elements*
- *Capability to exchange data using a STEP AP-239 compliant DEX*
- *Capability to affirm that system model elements conform to SAVI consistency checking guidelines or to spell out why and where they are inconsistent*

4. ACKNOWLEDGMENT

The assistance of all current members of the SAVI team is gratefully acknowledged.

5. REFERENCES

[1] SAE AIR 6110, December 2011. *Contiguous Aircraft/ System Development Process Example.* SAE Internatioinal, Warrendale, PA 15096-0001, USA. http://standard/sae.org/arp6110/.

[2] Cofer, D. D. 2011. *Design Documentation Guided Tour: Complexity-Reducing Design Patterns for Cyber-Physical Systems.* Technical Report. DARPA TTO/META Contract FA8650-10-C-7081 (September 20, 2011). https://wiki.sei.cmu.edu/aadl/images/3/3e/RC_META_Guide d_Tour.pdf .

Reddo - A Model Driven Engineering Toolset for Embedded Software Development [extended abstract]

Steven Doran
Northrop Grumman Corporation
B160-2
1100 W Hollyvale St, Azusa, CA 91702
(626) 812-1000
steven.doran@ngc.com

Stephanie E. August, PhD
Loyola Marymount University
MS-8145
Los Angeles, CA 90045-2659
(310) 338-5973
saugust@lmu.edu

ABSTRACT
This paper presents the Reddo Toolset as a study into MDE with a specific emphasis in embedded software application development. The goal of the Reddo Toolset is to determine whether if MDE can reduce the implementation time and improve the reliability of embedded software applications development by providing an auto source code generator tailored for the strict embedded hardware and timing requirements. The paper highlights the use of Reddo to design and implement a satellite simulator with a single payload as a case study.

Categories and Subject Descriptors
D. Software, **D.2** SOFTWARE ENGINEERING, **D.2.3** Coding Tools and Techniques, **Subjects:** Object-oriented programming

General Terms
Model Driven Engineering (MDE)

Keywords
Real-time programming, embedded, case study

1. INTRODUCTION
Over the past several years there has been a growing interest in Model Driven Engineering (MDE) from both academia and commercial entities as a method to reduce the cost and complexity of developing software applications for large complex systems. Most of this interest into MDE has not focused in the deployment embedded software applications due to the limited hardware and software resource requirements imposed on embedded software applications. The Reddo Project was developed as a study into MDE with a specific emphasis in embedded software application development. The goal of the Reddo Project is to determine whether if MDE can reduce the implementation time and improve the reliability of embedded software applications development by providing an auto source code generator tailored for the strict embedded hardware and timing requirements. To test Reddo's ability to generate successful embedded applications from MDE models, a "code off" case study was chosen to put Reddo against an experienced embedded software developer using traditional methods of embedded application development. The case study was a satellite simulator with restrictive hardware, software, and

timing requirements. Qualification testing was executed against both versions of the satellite simulators, and points were deducted if any requirement failed during qualification testing. Comparisons metrics such as total implementation time and number of generated defects between the Reddo generated source code and the traditional method of embedded software development was also used to determine the overall winner of the case study.

2. THE REDDO TOOLSET DEVELOPMENT APPROACH
The Reddo Toolset was developed as a prototype that supports the following functionality: 1) Ability to build a graphical UML model of an embedded application with a core framework for real-time scheduling of tasks, I/O Processing, and inter-model communication, 2) Auto generation of Ada source code from UML models, 3) Successfully execution of auto generated source code on an embedded device without manual source code modification, and 4) Native support for one embedded device.

The Ada programming language was selected as the programming language for source code generation due to Ada's advantages in real-time and concurrency support over other popular programming languages such as C/C++ or Java

2.1 The Reddo Integrated Design Environment (IDE)
The graphical Integrated Design Environment (IDE) for the Reddo Toolset was adopted from the ArgoUML4 open source project. ArgoUML source code was selected due to its mature development and extensive MDE functionality. ArgoUML was developed under the open source FreeBSD license that allows for modification and tailoring of the ArgoUML source code. Adopting ArgoUML saved time over developing a new IDE application specific for the Reddo Toolset.

2.2 The Reddo Auto Source Code Generator
The Reddo auto source code generator translates the XMI file generated by the Reddo graphical environment into source code. The auto source code generator is a stand-alone executable written in the Ada 2005 programming language.

2.3 The Reddo Toolset Framework
The Reddo Toolset Framework is a set of built-in classes that provide common functionality for project development. The Framework classes are represented as reusable abstractions of meta data wrapped in a well-defined Application Programming Interface (API). The user of the Reddo Toolset does not have the ability to modify or override the functionality of the framework classes. The purpose of the Reddo Toolset Framework provides

users of the Reddo Toolset a proven, off- the-shelf set of tools to aid in their system design and development. Using the Framework API's reduces the total time required to implement an embedded application. To incorporate Reddo Toolset Framework classes into an existing project, the framework classes must be added as interface classes.

3. CONVERSION OF UML META DATA TO SOURCE CODE USING THE REDDO TOOLSET

The Reddo Toolset includes two main components: (1) A graphical environment and (2) auto source code generator. The user of the Reddo Toolset uses the graphical environment to create a high level UML abstraction model of their embedded application. Once the UML abstraction model for their embedded application is complete, the user exports the model data into an XMI file. The XMI file is used by the auto source code generator in the generation of the source code. The auto source code generator, called the Reddo Source Code Generator (SCG) parses the exported XMI file generated from the Reddo IDE in the generation of source code.

Each type of UML diagram represents unique aspects of the system design. The SCG uses a layered approach using the meta data in each UML diagram to translate the UML meta data to source code. Below is the list of UML diagrams the SCG uses in its translation:

Layer 1 - Class Diagrams - Class diagrams describes the structure of a system by showing the system level classes with attributes, operations, or methods. The SCG creates system-level classes from the Class diagram meta data.

Layer 2 - Collaboration Diagrams - Collaboration diagrams describe the relationship between system level classes. The SCG configures each system level class's imports from the Collaboration diagram meta data.

Layer 3 - Activity Diagrams - Activity diagrams describes the activity within a class's method. The SCG uses the Activity diagram meta data to build the programming logic in a method within a class.

4. RESULTS OF THE "CODE OFF" CASE STUDY

The target embedded device for the Satellite Simulator was a Single Board Computer (SBC) with a Citrix based CPU, 640 megabytes of Random Access Memory (RAM), and a real-time clock. The operating system used was an embedded version of the Linux operating system. The amount of time required by both the Reddo Toolset and the traditional method to generate the satellite simulator's UML diagrams was the same. This result was expected since there is no discernible difference in generating UML diagrams using the Reddo Toolset. The advantage of the Reddo Toolset appeared during source code generation. The traditional software development approach requires the developer to create source code from scratch. The Reddo Toolset developer generated the satellite simulators source code by executing the Reddo's auto source code generator. The integration time using both the Reddo Toolset and traditional software development was the same. As with the creation of the UML diagrams, there was no advantage using the Reddo Toolset for integration testing. There were no defects found during qualification testing of the two satellite simulators. This was attributed to the experience of both Software Engineers participated in the case study. However, this result demonstrated the maturity of the Reddo Toolset. Finally, the Reddo Toolset had a significant advantage in the time between concept and deployment of the satellite simulator. The traditional software development approach required four times from concept to deployment compared to the Reddo Toolset.

5. CONCLUSION

The code off was a simple case study to demonstrate the ability of the Reddo Toolset to auto generates source code from UML meta data for embedded applications. As was demonstrated by the case study, the Reddo Toolset was able to implement the satellite simulator in less time and with the same system performance as an experienced software engineer using the traditional software development method.

6. REFERENCES

[1] Bowman, M., Debray, S. K Huber, B. S. A. P. F., and Philipps, J. Model based development of embedded systems. Advances in Object-Oriented Information Systems (2002)

[2] Schmidt, D. C. Guest Editor's Introduction: Model Driven Engineering. Computer (February 2006)

[3] Simonyan, S. A. S. D. C. C. S. K. M. S. M. Lessons learned in the current application of Model Driven Engineering. Ground System Architectures Workshop (2010)

Building Confidence in System Behavior

John Goodenough
Software Engineering Institute
Carnegie Mellon University
Pittsburgh, PA 15213
1-412-268-6391
jbg@sei.cmu.edu

ABSTRACT

If the use of Ada (or SPARK or some other tool) increases our confidence in the behavior of high integrity software systems, why does it do so? What do we mean by confidence, and what is a justified basis for asserting some level of confidence? In this talk, I'll address some recent research on the potential value of thinking about confidence in terms of eliminative induction, assurance cases, and confidence maps.

Categories and Subject Descriptors

K.6.4 [**Management of Computing and Information Systems**]: System Management—quality assurance; D.2.4 [**Software Engineering**]: Software/Program Verification—reliability, validation

General Terms

Management, Design, Reliability, Verification.

Keywords

Assurance cases; confidence maps; safety cases; assurance.

1. ACKNOWLEDGMENTS

This material is based upon work funded and supported by the Department of Defense under Contract No. FA8721-05-C-0003 with Carnegie Mellon University for the operation of the Software Engineering Institute, a federally funded research and development center.

Any opinions, findings and conclusions or recommendations expressed in this material are those of the author(s) and do not necessarily reflect the views of the United States Department of Defense.

This material has been approved for public release and unlimited distribution. DM-0000616

Compositional Verification of a Medical Device System*

Anitha Murugesan
Department of Computer
Science and Engineering
University of Minnesota
200 Union Street,
Minneapolis, Minnesota 55455
anitha@cs.umn.edu

Michael W. Whalen
Department of Computer
Science and Engineering
University of Minnesota
200 Union Street,
Minneapolis, Minnesota 55455
whalen@cs.umn.edu

Sanjai Rayadurgam
Department of Computer
Science and Engineering
University of Minnesota
200 Union Street,
Minneapolis, Minnesota 55455
rsanjai@cs.umn.edu

Mats P.E. Heimdahl
Department of Computer
Science and Engineering
University of Minnesota
200 Union Street,
Minneapolis, Minnesota 55455
heimdahl@cs.umn.edu

ABSTRACT

Complex systems are by necessity hierarchically organized. Decomposition into subsystems allows for intellectual control, as well as enabling different subsystems to be created by distinct teams. This decomposition affects both requirements and architecture. The architecture describes the structure and this affects how requirements "flow down" to each subsystem. Moreover, discoveries in the design process may affect the requirements. Demonstrating that a complex system satisfies its requirements when the subsystems are composed is a challenging problem.

In this paper, we present a medical device case example where we apply an iterative approach to architecture and verification based on software architectural models. We represent the hierarchical composition of the system in the Architecture Analysis & Design Language (AADL), and use an extension to the AADL language to describe the requirements at different levels of abstraction for compositional verification. The component-level behavior for the model is described in Simulink/Stateflow. We assemble proofs of system level properties by using the Simulink Design Verifier to establish component-level properties and an open-source plug-in for the OSATE AADL environment to perform the compositional verification of the architecture. This combination of verification tools allows us to iteratively explore design and verification of detailed behavioral models, and to scale formal analysis to large software systems.

*This work has been partially supported by NSF grants CNS-0931931 and CNS-1035715.

Categories and Subject Descriptors

D.2.1 [**Software Engineering**]: Requirements/Specifications—*Methodologies - Requirements flow down*; D.2.4 [**Software Engineering**]: Software/Program Verification—*Formal methods; Model checking*

Keywords

Compositional Verification; System Decomposition; Cyber Physical Systems

1. INTRODUCTION

Software is ubiquitous in safety-critical systems, which have the potential to cause loss of life, injury, or other serious damage to property and environment. The size and complexity of this software continues to grow, making it ever more difficult to capture the correct requirements, design the software correctly, and verify to a high level of confidence that we have the right requirements and that the software indeed satisfies those requirements. To make design and construction possible, such a complex system is typically organized as a composition of subsystems that can themselves be further decomposed if necessary. This hierarchical aspect of design is of crucial importance; it allows the complexity of the entire system to be managed through partitioning and abstraction.

One question related to this decomposition of a system is whether a constraint is considered a requirement or a design decision. The answer depends largely on one's perspective: design decisions at one level of abstraction naturally become requirements on the next lower level of abstraction. This dichotomy illustrates the natural interplay between system/software architecture and requirements refinement. In research and in practice, however, software architecture and software requirements tend to be quite distinct, supported by different research communities, tools and techniques. Based on Nuseibeh's TwinPeaks idea [31], we advocate a close and iterative relationship between software requirements and architecture [36]. Given adequate tools, this approach allows quick iterations between requirements and design, and supports efficient verification of the *adequacy* of the decomposition, i.e., the requirements allocated to the subsystems and their architectural connections imply the requirements at the next higher level of abstraction.

In this paper, we describe an application of this approach to the control software of a medical device—a Patient Controlled Analgesia Infusion Pump. We model the system architecture in the Architectural Analysis & Design Language (AADL) [33] and the component level behavior in the Simulink and Stateflow languages [24, 25]. For requirements, we start from textual system requirements expressed in natural language (English). We formalize these requirements using an extension of the AADL language that supports specification of formal textual requirements for systems at different levels of the system hierarchy within the AADL model. Currently our extension allows specification of temporal logic invariants using a structuring mechanism similar to the Property Specification Language (PSL) [16]. We then use the AGREE framework [5]—a compositional verification framework developed for AADL verification by Rockwell Collins and University of Minnesota,—to prove that system requirements are established, given the architectural structure of the system and the requirements allocated to sub-systems in the architecture.

The sample system used in this paper is a medical device— a Generic Patient Controlled Analgesia (GPCA) infusion pump system [1]. Infusion pumps are medical devices used to accurately infuse liquids into a patient's bloodstream. Medical devices, such as infusion pumps, are suitable systems to explore since they are generally safety-critical and the maturity level of the V&V process has often been insufficient to ensure the safety and overall quality of the devices. Infusion pumps have been involved in numerous incidents that have resulted in harm to the patient. The US Food and Drug Administration (FDA), through its Infusion Pump Improvement Initiative, has sought to pro-actively increase the safety of these devices by establishing additional regulatory requirements for infusion pump manufacturers. In this context, the research community—in collaboration with the FDA—is exploring various methods to improve the safety of infusion pump systems. Our aim is to contribute to this initiative by building a powerful and scalable proof framework and evaluate its effectiveness by applying it to various medical devices.

We have modeled the GPCA architecture using AADL and the behavior of the architectural components in Simulink and Stateflow. We are in the process of formalizing and proving the GPCA system and software requirements. We have currently formalized and proved a significant fraction (about 30%) of the top-level software requirements using compositional verification. We expect to complete the formalization and verification of the remainder in the near future (we are aware of no technical hurdles; it is simply a matter of time). The component-level proofs and architectural proofs are established efficiently: our component level models require ≈4 minutes to prove and the architectural proofs are in the order of 2 seconds.

In any development effort, we expect that requirements, architectures, and components will co-evolve as the project progresses. Requirements naturally influence the architecture and design, architectural consideration may expose the need for new or modified requirements, and the verification

efforts are likely to reveal flaws in the requirements as well as the architecture and design [28]. We also anticipate that verification of different parts may involve formal evidence (for example, proof) as well as empirical and analytic evidence (for example, testing, inspections, etc.). Given appropriate tools, it may be possible to perform top-to-bottom system level formal proofs; however, the approach is designed to support selective proofs for the portions of the system that are most critical, or that can be easily addressed with automated tools. Finally, we have attempted to use established notations for component-level behavior (Simulink and Stateflow) and architectural description (AADL) supported by commercial or open-source tools. Our hope is to demonstrate that this approach is a reasonable and cost-effective *engineering* solution for construction of safety-critical systems; an approach that could be readily adopted into industrial practice.

2. TARGET SYSTEM

Infusion pumps are medical cyber physical systems used for controlled delivery of liquid drugs into a patient's body according to a physician's prescription (the set of instructions that governs infusion rates for a medication). These pumps may be classified into various kinds depending on their features, construction, and usage. Patient-Controlled Analgesia (PCA) pumps are generally equipped with a feature that allows patients to self-administer a controlled amount of drug (a patient-bolus), typically a pain medication.

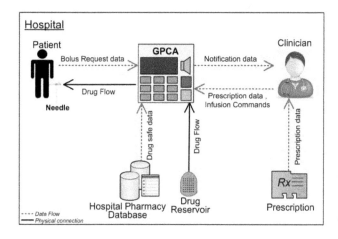

Figure 1: Environment—GPCA System Overview

Figure 1 shows an external intravenous Generic Patient Controlled Analgesia (GPCA) device in a typical usage environment, a hospital or a clinic. In an infusion system, the clinician operates the GPCA device, programs the prescription information, loads the drug, connects the device with the patient, and responds to exceptional conditions that occur during the therapy. The patient receives the medication from the device through an intravenous needle. The patient can self-administer prescribed amounts of additional drug by requesting a bolus, a request usually done by pressing a bolus request button accessible at the patient's bed. The hospital pharmacy database is a repository that stores manufacturer provided drug information (for example, upper limits on infusion rates for a specific drug).

In short, the GPCA system has three primary functions (1) deliver the drug based on the prescribed schedule and patient requests, (2) prevent hazards that may arise during its usage, and (3) monitor and notify the clinician of any exceptional conditions encountered. In this paper we will focus our attention on the architecture and behavior of the software portion of the overall GPCA system.

3. ARCHITECTURE AND REQUIREMENTS

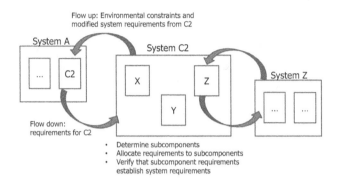

Figure 2: Requirements and Architectural Decomposition

Once systems become sufficiently complex, they are decomposed into subsystems that are created by several distinct teams. Thus, the requirements on the system as a whole must be decomposed and allocated to each of the subsystems. This decomposition touches both requirements and architecture, since the architecture describes the structure of the decomposition, and this will affect how requirements "flow down" to each subsystem. We believe that requirements should be organized into hierarchies that follow the architectural decomposition of the system because the act of decomposing a system into components induces a requirements analysis effort in which we need to ascertain whether the requirements allocated to subcomponents in the architecture are sufficient to establish the system-level requirements. Equally importantly, we need to determine whether any assumptions on a component's environment made when allocating requirements to that component can be established. This is shown informally in Figure 2. As we begin to allocate requirements to components, we may find that the architecture we have chosen simply cannot satisfy the system-level requirements. This may cause us to re-architect the system to allow us to meet the system level requirement, levy additional constraints on the external environment, or renegotiate the system-level requirement [36].

The GPCA is a physical device that contains an infusion pump, a user interface containing an input panel as well as audio and visual alarms, a variety of sensors related to the current status of the device, and a microcontroller containing software to control the device. For the software architecture, we have chosen to largely mimic the structure of the physical system. Thus, the major sub-systems include (1) Alarm—responsible for monitoring exceptional conditions and raising alerts to avoid hazards to the patient, (2) Infusion— responsible for determining the current mode of

the system and commanding the flow of drug out of the device, (3) Mode—responsible for managing the top-level operating mode of the system, and (4) Logging—responsible for logging the status of the device. These subsystems are shown in Figure 3. As we are currently focusing on the software controller, we are not yet describing the user-interface portion of the GPCA software.

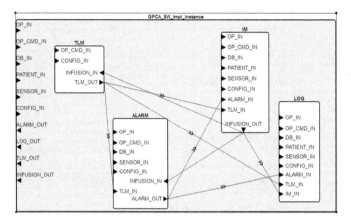

Figure 3: Software architecture of the GPCA controller

To illustrate the architectural decomposition with respect to the software requirements for the GPCA pump, consider the following system level requirement:

> *When performing infusion, if the remaining volume of drug in the reservoir drops below the empty-drug-threshold, the GPCA Pump shall raise visual and aural alarms and stop infusion.*

When allocated to software, this requirement addresses the inputs and outputs of the software (as opposed to the physical phenomena addressed in the system requirement):

> *When in the infusing-mode, if the estimated drug remaining in the drug reservoir drops below the empty drug threshold (estimated-drug-remaining < empty-drug-threshold), the GPCA software shall issue the visual-alarm and aural-alarm commands, and stop the infusion.*

Since the particular infusion pump we are modeling does not measure the volume of drug infused, the remaining drug volume is estimated by subtracting the estimated volume of drug infused from the initial volume of the drug contained in the reservoir.

The software requirement is further decomposed and allocated to the *Alarms* (ALARM in Figure 3) and *Infusion Manager* (IM) components. Here, the solution is to require the Alarms component to monitor the estimated remaining drug and—when it drops below the threshold—raise a critical alarm:

> *When in the infusing-mode, if the estimated drug remaining in the drug reservoir is below the empty drug threshold (estimated-drug-remaining < empty-drug-threshold), the Alarms subsystem shall set the highest-level-alarm to 4 (critical alarm) and set the empty-drug-alarm indicator in current-alarm.*

The Alarms subsystem defines four levels of severity from level 1 (informational) to level 4 (critical). These levels are used by the rest of the system to determine correct infusing and logging behavior. The Infusion Manager component is responsible for receiving the notification from the Alarm component and signaling the hardware to stop infusion by commanding the flow rate to zero:

The infusion manager shall stop infusion whenever a critical alarm occurs (highest-level-alarm=4)

In addition, the Infusion Manager component is responsible for estimating the remaining reservoir volume. If the sub-component requirements are adequate, it will be possible to demonstrate that the higher level software requirement is actually met by our design.

In the full system, there are dozens of requirements allocated to software relating to the correct behavior of the system. The requirements involve correct diagnosis of sensor and actuator failures, tolerances for infusion, logging, self test, and many other aspects. An interested reader can examine the full GPCA requirements at the following web site: http://crisys.cs.umn.edu/gpca.shtml.

3.1 Architectural Modeling and AADL

In order to document, visualize, and analyze the architecture of the GPCA system, we need to model it. When modeling embedded safety-critical systems such as the GPCA, it is desirable to have an architectural model that supports descriptions of both hardware and software components and their interactions. We need to document component interfaces, interconnections between components, and requirements on components, without describing the implementations of those components. At the leaf level, component implementations are defined separately using model-based development tools or by traditional programming languages, as appropriate.

The Architecture Analysis and Description Language (AADL) is a notation that suits these needs. AADL supports many of the constructs needed to model embedded systems such as processes, threads, devices (sensors and actuators), processors, buses, and memory. Furthermore, it contains an extension mechanism (called an *annex*) that can be used to extend the language to support additional features, such as requirements modeling. AADL, now an SAE standard [33], is a textual language that can be expressed graphically and is accompanied by a UML profile. AADL includes constructs that describe both software and hardware components, as well as mapping software components to physical resources and the devices with which they communicate. It allows for specification of interfaces for flow of control and data. The basic building block of this notation is a component, defined by its category (hardware, software, or composite), type (how the component interacts with the outside world), and its implementation (an instance of the component type). Note that there can be many instances of one component type. For example, highly available systems often have redundant computing resources to support failover; these can be represented as instances of a single component type. Our current GPCA example does not have redundant processing elements, but these may be added in the future.

The graphical representation in AADL of the GPCA software architecture is shown in Figure 3. The

GPCA_SW_Impl_Instance describes an instantiation of the GPCA_SW system. In the GPCA model, inputs and outputs are defined along the left side of the figure. We group the inputs from different sources: operator inputs (OP_IN), operator commands (OP_CMD_IN), drug database inputs (DB_IN), patient inputs (PATIENT_IN), sensor inputs (SENSOR_IN), and system configuration inputs (CONFIG_IN), in order to simplify signal routing throughout the model. In the current model, these six input sources contain 76 different scalar signals. Connections between components can be *immediate* (visualized by lines in the diagram containing the $>>$ symbol) or *delayed* (visualized by "plain" lines). The designation determines whether communication between components will happen in the same time frame or delayed by one time frame; immediate connections induce data-dependency constraints on scheduling of components. Given a deterministic single-processor system, these correspond to immediate connections and $1/z$-delayed connections in Simulink/Stateflow. To remove clutter from the figure, we do not show connections from the subsystems to the system boundary; the inputs and outputs of the subsystems are connected to the inports and outports of the system with the same name.

AADL is supported by a growing number of tools, including tools that support editing and import/export of AADL models, as well as tools that allow one to analyze different aspects of the model—correctness of the connections, component resource usage within limits, etc. However, AADL does not have a built-in means of associating requirements with different components within the architecture, nor does it have support reasoning about requirements. The AGREE framework addresses these issues by adding support for requirements capture and formal verification (described in more detail in the next section) to the OSATE AADL tool.

3.2 Reasoning about Architectural Models with AGREE

To convincingly argue that a system has the desired effect in its environment (the system satisfies its requirements), Hammond et al. developed the notion of a Satisfaction Argument, based on Jackson and Zave's World and the Machine model [13, 17]. This approach attempts to establish that system requirements hold through an argument involving (i) the specification of the system behavior and (ii) assumptions about the domain of the system.

To formalize satisfaction arguments, assume-guarantee contracts [27] provide an appropriate mechanism for capturing the information needed from other modeling domains to reason about system-level properties. In this formulation, guarantees correspond to component requirements, and assumptions correspond to the environmental constraints that are used in verifying the component requirements. For formally verified components, assumptions are assertions or invariants on component inputs that are used in the proof process. A contract specifies precisely the information that is needed to reason about the component's interaction with other parts of the system. Furthermore, the contract mechanism supports a hierarchical decomposition of the verification process that follows the natural hierarchy in the system model.

In our framework, we use the past-time operator subset of *past-time linear temporal logic* (PLTL) [19]. Temporal logics like PLTL include operators for reasoning about the

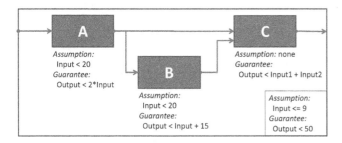

Figure 4: Toy Architecture with Properties

behavior of propositions over a sequence of instants in time. For example, to say that property P is always true at every instant in time (i.e., it is "globally" true), one would write $G(P)$, where G stands for "globally".

Figure 4 illustrates the compositional verification conditions for a toy example. In this example, we would like to establish at the system (S) level that the output signal is always less than 50, given that the input signal is less than 10. We can prove this using the assumptions and guarantees provided by the subcomponents A, B, and C that are organized hierarchically. This figure shows one layer of decomposition, but the idea generalizes to arbitrarily many layers. We want to be able to compose proofs starting from the leaf components (those whose implementation is specified outside of the architecture model) recursively through all the layers of the architecture.

The correctness obligations are the form $G(H(A) \Rightarrow P)$, which informally means that it is always the case that if assumption A has been true from the beginning of the execution up until this instant (A is *historically* true), then guarantee P is true. For the obligation in Figure 4, our goal is to prove the formula $G(H(A_S) \Rightarrow P_S)$ given the contracted behavior $G(H(A_c) \Rightarrow P_c)$ for each component c within the system. To prove the obligation, we establish generic *verification conditions* that together are sufficient to establish the goal formula. In the example, this means that for the system S we want to prove that $Output < 50$ assuming that $Input < 10$ and the contracts for components A, B, and C are satisfied. For a system with n components there are $n + 1$ verification conditions: one for each component and one for the system as a whole. The component verification conditions establish that the assumptions of each component are implied by the system level assumptions and the properties of its sibling components. For this system the verification conditions generated would be:

$$G(H(A_S) \Rightarrow A_A)$$
$$G(H(A_S \wedge P_A) \Rightarrow A_B)$$
$$G(H(A_S \wedge P_A \wedge P_B) \Rightarrow A_C)$$
$$G(H(A_S \wedge P_A \wedge P_B \wedge P_C) \Rightarrow P_S)$$

In general, these verification conditions may be cyclic, but if there is a delay element in the cycle we can use induction over time as in [27]. The system level verification condition shows that the system guarantees follow from the system assumptions and the properties of each subcomponent. This is essentially an expansion of the original goal, $G(H(A_S) \Rightarrow P_S)$, with the additional information obtained from each component.

3.3 GPCA System Architecture and Requirements in AADL/AGREE

AADL distinguishes between a *system*, which describe the input/output interface of an AADL aggregate, and *system implementations*, which describe the internal structure of the system. Each system type may have several implementations. We define requirements contracts in a *system* because requirements are defined over the input/output interface of the component and should not be defined in terms of implementation details. However, we perform proofs at the *system implementation* level, where we can use the contracts of subcomponents and their architectural relationship to establish system level properties. So, in Figure 3, we are examining the implementation of the *GPCA_SW* system, which is defined in terms of *TLM, ALARM, IM,* and *LOG* systems. The structure of the subsystems is hidden; instead we prove the obligations for GPCA_SW using the contracts defined by the subsystems. For each layer of the architecture, we establish, for each implementation of a system, that the implementation meets the requirements of the system defined in the layer. Transitively, we thus establish that the requirements of the top-level system are proved given that the properties of the lowest layer leaf-level components are true.

An example of the notation for the AGREE framework is shown in Figure 5. The language is based on Property Specification Language (PSL) [16] and defines a Lustre language [11] "flavor" for the PSL Boolean layer expressions and definitions. Lustre is a synchronous dataflow language that describes the behavior of a system through a set of equations, and it can be viewed as a textual analogue to Simulink block diagrams. In this notation, it is possible to define constants, local variables, reusable fragments of temporal logic (called properties), and to make guarantees (called assertions) and assumptions. In specifications, we can reference values of input and output ports; additionally, we can describe stateful relationships between variables using the 'prev' expression, which provides the value of a variable from the previous step of execution of the system (the second argument to this expression provides its value in the initial state). Given this notation, it is possible to encode the requirements that we described informally in the previous section. For example, the empty reservoir requirement from the previous section is formally specified in REQ 59. The structure of contracts is the same for the subcomponents, though of course the interfaces and properties are specialized to the functionality of each subcomponent.

4. BEHAVIORAL MODELING

In the work described in this paper, the detailed component behavior for the GPCA System has been modeled in Simulink and Stateflow. Simulink and Stateflow are developed by MathWorks [22]. Simulink is a data flow graphical language as well as a tool for modeling and simulating dynamic systems (both the language and the tool are generally referred to as Simulink). Stateflow is a state-based notation similar to David Harel's Statecharts notation [14] (again, Stateflow also refers to the tool). Both Simulink and Stateflow are tightly integrated in the MATLAB environment and can, as mentioned earlier, refer to other languages available in the environment. Although both Stateflow and Simulink, in our opinion, have many problems with their semantics (such as the lack of proper type systems, the event seman-

```
system GPCA_SW
  features
    OP_IN: in data port DATATYPES::Operator_Inputs.Impl;
    OP_CMD_IN: in data port DATATYPES::Operator_Commands.Impl;
    DB_IN: in data port DATATYPES::Drug_Database_Inputs.Impl;
    PATIENT_IN: in data port DATATYPES::Patient_Inputs.Impl;
    SENSOR_IN: in data port DATATYPES::Device_Sensor_Inputs.Impl;
    CONFIG_IN: in data port DATATYPES::Device_Configuration_Inputs.Impl;
    ALARM_OUT: out data port DATATYPES::Alarm_Outputs.Impl;
    LOG_OUT: out data port DATATYPES::Log_Outputs.Impl;
    TLM_OUT : out data port DATATYPES::Top_Level_Mode_Outputs.Impl;
    INFUSION_OUT: out data port DATATYPES::Infusion_Manager_Outputs.Impl;
  properties
    PSL_Properties::Contract => "
    -- Constants
      const IM_MODE_OFF : int = 0;
      const IM_MODE_IDLE : int = 1;
      const IM_MODE_PAUSED : int = 2;
      ...

      -- macros
      property in_off = INFUSION_OUT.Current_System_Mode = IM_MODE_OFF;
      property in_idle = INFUSION_OUT.Current_System_Mode = IM_MODE_IDLE;
      property in_paused = INFUSION_OUT.Current_System_Mode = IM_MODE_PAUSED;
      ...


      ----------------------------------------------------------------
      -- SYSTEM REQUIREMENTS
      ----------------------------------------------------------------

      ...
      -- REQ 4 :
      property RE_system_on_implies_idle =
        ((not prev(TLM_OUT.System_On, true) and (TLM_OUT.System_On)) => in_idle);
      assert RE_system_on_implies_idle;
      ...
      -- REQ 6 :
      property mode_off_implies_infusion_rate_zero =
          in_off => (INFUSION_OUT.Commanded_Flow_Rate = 0);
      assert mode_off_implies_infusion_rate_zero;
      ...
      -- REQ 59:
      property empty_reservoir_implies_no_flow =
      ((((prev(INFUSION_OUT.Reservoir_Volume, 0)) < CONFIG_IN.Empty_Reservoir_Val)
        and prev(INFUSION_OUT.Infusing, false)) =>
        (INFUSION_OUT.Commanded_Flow_Rate = 0));
      assert empty_reservoir_implies_no_flow;
      ...
      ----------------------------------------------------------------
      -- SYSTEM LEVEL ASSUMPTIONS
      ----------------------------------------------------------------
      assume DB_IN.flow_rate_kvo > 0 ;
      assume CONFIG_IN.audio_level_val > 0 ;
      assume CONFIG_IN.empty_reservoir_val > 0 ;
    ----------------------------------------------------------------
    -- End of Infusion Manager Contract
    ----------------------------------------------------------------
    ";
end GPCA_SW;
```

Figure 5: Portions of GPCA AADL/Agree Model

tics in Stateflow, the distinction between transition actions and condition actions, etc.), they are by far the most widely used notations in industry and suit our modeling needs well.

Furthermore, since our goal is to demonstrate the power of formal reasoning, it is essential to have verification support for the behavioral modeling notation. The MathWorks now supports a plug-in formal verification tool, the Simulink Design Verifier [23], for verification of Simulink and Stateflow behavioral models.

Finally, since one of the goals with the effort described in this paper was to illustrate how to perform architectural modeling, behavioral modeling, and compositional verification in practice, our aim was to work with commercially supported and/or mature open source tools so that adopting our work in industrial settings would have a low threshold. Thus, Simulink, Stateflow, and AGREE were natural choices.

4.1 Alarms Component

The Alarms component monitors the system for any exceptional conditions, prioritizes conditions if there are multiple simultaneous exceptional conditions, and raises visual/audio notifications depending on the situation. Figure 6 shows the top level model of the Alarms component. The dashed "roundangles" indicate state-machines that exist in parallel but that will execute in the sequence indicated by the sequence numbers (in this case, CheckAlarms and then Notification). The CheckAlarms state-machine determines which alarms to raise based on the the current information of the system. Figure 7 shows the behavioral model of the reservoir empty alarms feature, one of the sub-states of CheckAlarms state-machine. The behavior is relatively simple: if infusion is in progress (information gathered from the Infusion Manager component discussed below), and the estimated volume remaining in the reservoir (also from the Infusion Manager) is less than the Empty Reservoir threshold, the reservoir is considered empty and the alarm will be raised. In the Alarms module there are currently 18 different alarms that can be raised. The alarms range from low criticality alarms that amount to an on screen notification to the clinician and no disruption of the therapy, to highly critical alarms (such as Empty Reservoir or Air In Line) that necessitate a visual and aural notification (determined by the Notification state-machine) as well as suspension of therapy.

4.2 Infusion Manager Component

The Infusion Manager is responsible for maintaining the state of the infusion of drug into the patient and, based on the therapy selected, determining the appropriate flow-rate for the infusion. In addition, the Infusion Manager is responsible for estimating the total volume infused and the remaining reservoir volume. The top level of the Infusion Manager can be seen in Figure 8.

Initially, the Infusion Manager is idle and no infusion is taking place. After the pump has been configured, that is, the various infusion parameters have been set, the clinician can commence the delivery of an infusion therapy as shown in Figure 8; Figure 9 shows the details of the therapy behavior. When delivering therapy, the pump may be actively delivering drug (ACTIVE) or drug delivery may be suspended (PAUSED). System may be PAUSED for two reasons; (1) a critical alarm may have been raised necessitating the cessation of drug delivery (information from the Alarms subsystem), or (2) the clinician has requested a pause to perform some action.

When the pump is delivering therapy (in the ACTIVE state), this particular version of the GPCA can provide three types of therapy: (1) a basal infusion rate that is the basis for the therapy, (2) a higher patient requested bolus rate that is limited in duration and frequency (to prevent patient self-inflicted overdoses), and (3) a clinician programmed intermittent bolus regime where the patient gets an extra dose of drug at regularly scheduled intervals (see Figure 10). Depending on various conditions, the infusion pump will switch between these delivery therapies. As an example, consider a scenario where the pump is delivering therapy at the basal flow rate. The patient requests a bolus dose and—if all preconditions are met—this therapy is turned on. In this case, the patient bolus takes precedence over all other therapies and the flow rate delivered to the patient is determined by the patient bolus rate. When the patient bolus has been delivered, the previous therapy is resumed. In this model, the prioritization of the various therapies is handled by the ARBITER state machine. The inclusion of an arbiter as well as the modeling of the various therapies as parallel state machines was done for clarity, modularity, and product family reasons; this structure makes it relatively easy to add additional therapies without causing ripple-effects throughout the model. The details and rationale related to the structuring of the behavioral models is outside the scope of this paper and has been discussed elsewhere [30].

4.3 Specification of Behavioral Requirements

The required properties of the architectural components is captured in AGREE using the past-time subset of past-time linear temporal logic—PLTL (Section 3.2). Unfortunately, the verification tools available for Simulink and Stateflow do not currently support this formalism for property specification. Naturally, it would be highly desirable if the property specification language was consistent throughout the modeling effort; this is a tool integration and engineering problem we have not yet addressed. Instead, we recapture the required component properties for verification in the Simulink Design Verifier. The Simulink Design Verifier requires all properties to be specified as Boolean expressions in one of the available MATLAB notations. For example, the empty reservoir property for the Alarms component depicted in Figure 11 is captured as a Simulink verification block. The input signals on the left side are the same inputs that are provided to the Alarms component capturing the component behavior (as discussed in the previous section). The gray circle containing a P (for property) indicates that the verification tools will attempt to verify that this Simulink block always generates a signal that is True; if the signal is ever False, the tools have revealed a property violation and will report a counterexample. The logic of the verification condition is in Figure 11 expressed using embedded MATLAB, a subset of the MATLAB computing language that supports efficient code generation for deployment in embedded systems.

Alternatively, the verification conditions could be captured using the Simulink or Stateflow notations. The same condition captured as a Simulink model can be seen in Figure 12.

In our work we have preferred using embedded MATLAB code. Capturing properties in this notation has several advantages. First, the property can be structured to closely resemble the natural language "shall" requirements in the requirement document as well as the PLTL properties used in AGREE. This closeness in structure reduces the opportunities for transcription mistakes and makes the properties easier to inspect. In the future, the translation between the AGREE properties and the Design Verifier properties will be automated. Second, the textual notations makes it easy to comment out properties as the verification process is underway (verifying all properties all the time may be a waste of time when there is one problematic property of interest). Finally, we have developed preference for the textual notation since we find it quicker and easier to create and maintain the required properties textually.

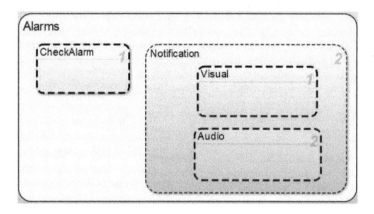

Figure 6: Alarm Behavioral Model Top-Level State Machine

Figure 7: Behavioral model of the reservoir empty alarms feature.

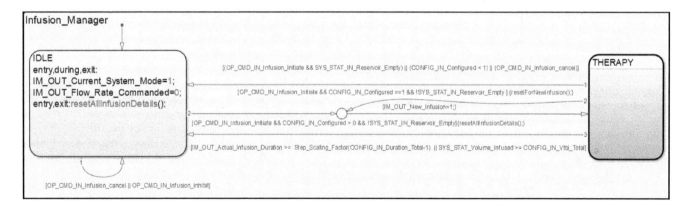

Figure 8: Infusion Manager Behavioral Model Top-Level State Machine

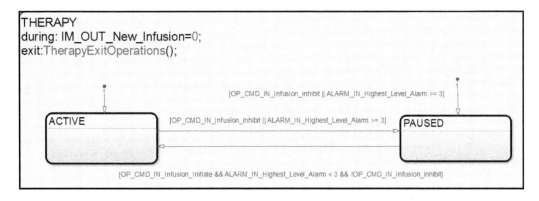

Figure 9: Therapy state machine.

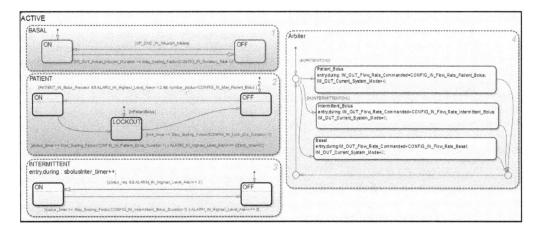

Figure 10: The three main therapies and the arbiter determining which one is in control of the pump.

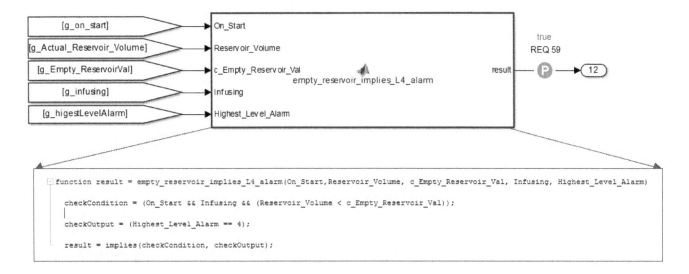

Figure 11: Alarm component property for Empty Reservoir check expressed in embedded MATLAB.

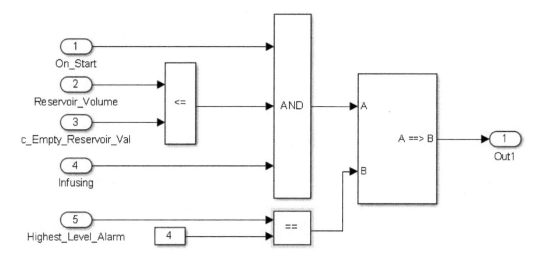

Figure 12: Alarm component property for Empty Reservoir check expressed in Simulink.

5. VERIFYING THE GPCA SYSTEM

To verify the GPCA system behavior, it is necessary to prove that the components satisfy their component-level requirements and that the component-level requirements are adequate to establish the system-level requirements for each level within the architectural hierarchy. These activities were performed in parallel, with one team member leading the component-level verification effort and another leading the architecture-level verification.

5.1 Verification Approach and Tools

For the verification effort of the GPCA model, we used two different model checking tools. For the Simulink/Stateflow verification, we used the Simulink Design Verifier (SLDV) [23], and for the architectural verification, we used the recently developed Rockwell Collins JKind tool[1]. Both of the tools use k-induction [34] algorithms implemented on top of a Satisfiability Modulo Theories (SMT) solver [8] to reason about infinite-state models involving real (rational) numbers and bounded or unbounded integers.

5.2 Verification Results

The verification results for our current analysis are shown in Table 1. Currently, we are analyzing component-level properties for the Alarms and Infusion Manager components (we expect to add properties related to logging and the top-level system modes in the near future). For composing analysis results, we are using AADL and the AGREE OSATE plug-in. All data gathering was performed on a Dell Latitude E6430 running Windows 7 64-bit edition with an Intel Core i7-3720QM CPU running at 2.60 GHz and 6 GB of RAM. For each slot in the table, we ran the verification three times and recorded the mean time (though variance was quite low between runs).

To evaluate the scalability of the architectural analysis, we also created a model in Simulink that contains all of the behavioral models in the AADL architectural model; we call the composite Simulink model the *monolithic model*. We can then check the scalability of the compositional vs. monolithic analysis by analyzing the same system twice:

Compositional Approach: In this approach, the component-level properties for the Alarms and Infusion Manager subsystems are proven using Simulink Design Verifier; these properties are then used to prove the system property.

Monolithic Approach: In this approach, the monolithic model containing the Alarms and Infusion Manager subsystems as well as the 19 system-level properties is analyzed using Simulink Design Verifier.

For the monolithic model, Simulink Design Verifier is unable to prove the current set of system-level properties within 60 minutes. For the compositional approach, the total time required for analysis is slightly under 5 minutes ($46.5 + 224.5 + 2 = 273$ seconds). Notably, the time required for the compositional portion of the analysis was only 2 seconds. As we add additional subsystems and additional functionality and proof obligations to the component-level models, we expect the difference in analysis time to become more pronounced.

6. DISCUSSION

In the process of conducting this case study, we gained some methodological insights towards model structuring and verification.

6.1 Model Structure

It is crucial to structure the component models carefully taking into consideration their various uses and evolution. Initially, we placed both the functional model and requirements models (properties) into the same Simulink model. However, we wanted the Simulink models to serve two important purposes—code-generation and verification. Also, we wanted the implementation of the component and the specification of the requirements for that component to be able to evolve in parallel, given that the input/output interface for the component is stable. To support these desires, we create three models for each component. For component foo, we create the model foo_functional.mdl to capture the detailed component behavior, foo_properties.mdl

---

[1]Available at: https://github.com/agacek/jkind

	Alarms Sub-System	Infusion Manager Sub-System	Monolithic Model	AADL Model
Number of Inputs	45	21	55	55
Number of Outputs	10	11	15	15
Number of Properties	11	15	19	19
Design Verifier Execution Time	46.5s	224.5s	>3600s (12/19 proved)	NA
AGREE Execution Time	NA	NA	NA	2s

Table 1: Verification Results

to capture the requirements for the component, and `foo_-verification.mdl` that connects the functional and requirements models. Eventually, given an AADL model containing the I/O structure and requirements allocated to the component, we plan to auto-generate the verification models. We intend to use the functional models to generate code using the MATLAB code-generation tools; code that can then be executed and tested on the target platform.

6.2 Debugging

The formalization effort found errors in requirements, architectural decomposition, and behavioral models. In terms of requirements, we found implicit assumptions, ambiguous textual requirements, and specifications that were not physically achievable (note that this is not a new insight [12, 28]). For example, we have various requirements related to under- and over-infusion, where at any instant an over- or under-infusion amount greater than a certain threshold vs. the current desired flow rate should trigger a critical alarm and stop infusion:

> SW3.4.5.21.2 The application shall validate during all infusion modes if the received flow rate is within programmed flow rate with flow rate precision of p % of the programmed flow rate of the respective infusion mode. The received flow rate shall never be more than MAX ml/hr above the prescribed flow rate + precision.

These requirements as written, however, are not achievable at start of infusion or during mode transitions (such as patient bolus), instants where the threshold changes via a step function and the pump requires a small amount of time to reach the set point. In the process of formalizing the requirement, we identified the problem.

The behavioral models contained the largest share of errors found by analysis, usually involving incorrectly specified boundary conditions. For example, incorrect default transitions (transitions that occur when a state machine is first entered) led to several instances where alarms were not correctly raised at the moment when the fault condition occurred.

In terms of architectural models, a significant error was found related to the structure of the decomposition that we had chosen for the system. A property closely related to the empty reservoir property discussed earlier is:

> No infusion shall occur while the drug reservoir is below the empty-drug-threshold for the drug in the reservoir.

This property is violated by the current model. The issue is that while the Infusion Manager will stop infusion if a critical alarm occurs, the Alarms subsystem will raise an alarm for empty reservoir only if the system is infusing. Therefore, the system must start infusion before the alarm will occur and cause infusion to stop. To fix this issue, we will split the Alarms system into a system status and alarms component. The status component will have an "okToInfuse" output to handle this case.

Both SLDV and the AGREE tool-set produce counterexamples when properties are violated. For behavioral models, tracing counterexamples is straightforward; they are test cases that can be run through the simulator for Simulink. On the other hand, if a counterexample occurs in AGREE, it is akin to a proof failure; the counterexample is a trace instance in which the subsystem properties and system assumptions were not strong enough to establish the system level property. In some cases, these counterexamples can be very difficult to debug—they may not correspond to actual executions of the system (because the component level properties are approximations of the actual system behavior) and therefore cannot be simulated. It will be important to provide engineers better tools with which to understand the relevance of different variables towards these counterexamples, to try to assign blame to subcomponents that likely contributed to the proof failure, and to perform some amount of automated strengthening by "opening the architectural boxes" and looking at the behavior of subcomponents. We are just beginning to investigate better tool support and engineering aspects of compositional reasoning as part of a NASA program that started in June 2013.

As mentioned above, the majority of faults have been found in the behavioral models, but the most difficult to fix involved the architectural decomposition. The benefit of having the ability to perform architectural verification is that these problems can be identified early in the verification process rather than in integration and system test phases.

6.3 Limitations

Our current approach to verification is restricted in several ways. First, AGREE currently only handles synchronous architectural models in which execution proceeds in a deterministic discrete sequence of steps. This model must be extended in order to deal with distributed computations where components do not share a common clock signal, or where messages between components are not guaranteed to be delivered and/or communication times may vary. Second, AGREE can verify only *invariants*, so liveness properties, such as *the system will eventually deliver a message*, cannot be specified in AGREE. In our experience, this is not as severe a limitation as it may seem. Most systems are concerned with *bounded liveness* in which an action must occur within a time interval; these properties can be written in AGREE.

The current analysis tools use *rationals* to model the behavior of real numbers; However, most software is implemented using floating point numbers. This can lead to unsoundness in our analysis of software that uses floating point arithmetic. Bit-precise floating point reasoning is an area of active research in the decision procedures community. As floating point decision procedures become integrated into SMT solvers, we will add support for accurate analysis of floating point numbers. Also, AGREE does not support trigonometric or non-linear functions. These can be approximated in some cases, but many of the interesting numeric properties of systems simply cannot be specified.

Finally, we are proving properties of *models*. The models that we are analyzing are used for code generation, and so describe a complete implementation of the functional behavior of the GPCA. However, the verification process that we describe will not catch errors in the MATLAB code generator or the C tool chain used to compile the generated code. In addition, external code such as "glue" code for communication with the actual sensors and actuators and (possibly) an RTOS are outside the scope of the model and will not be analyzed.

7. RELATED WORK

Compositional verification has attracted significant research attention because of its viability as a scalable technique for reasoning about complex systems. These techniques typically employ some form of an assume-guarantee approach: each component (or module) is shown to individually guarantee some desirable properties under certain assumptions about its environment, which includes other interacting components. These separate arguments are then combined in a logically coherent fashion to construct an argument that the full system satisfies its required properties under the given assumptions about its environment. When a formal technique such as model-checking is used to verify the properties, these "arguments" in essence are proofs of properties for the system models being verified.

Early efforts in such modular reasoning dealt with parallel programs that interact via message passing and shared variables [29, 18, 32] and recently in the context of *behavioral programming* frameworks [15]. In our present work, the focus is on verifying architectural models with behavioral components that interact through data flow and execute in some fixed sequential order at every computation step. The components themselves are modeled as extended finite state machines which are amenable to model-checking techniques. Event-based composition and verification of finite-state transition systems has been explored in the contexts of I/O automata [21], interface automata [6], Computational Tree Logics [3, 9], and in a process algebraic framework [2]. Hagen et al. discuss verification of safety properties of data-flow programs in Lustre using model-checking techniques that use an underlying SMT-solver [10]. In our present work we use the same SMT-based algorithm to verify properties in the AGREE framework.

McMillan describes a compositional approach to hardware verification where the component-level properties are verified using model-checkers, while the higher level properties are reasoned about using human assisted proof-techniques in a semi-automated fashion [26]. In the present work, we use a similar strategy for proving system properties by leveraging the human effort involved in system design for architectural decomposition as well as requirements allocation to sub-components. Such a division of labor between man and machine for full-system verification seems justified given that, in general, finding a good decomposition that is beneficial for verification is hard [4].

Simulink Design Verifier has been used to analyze cyber-physical system designs in the transportation domain [7]. Here, various properties of a train-tracking system are verified using the k-induction and bounded model-checking capabilities of the tools; the state-space explosion problem is addressed by adopting various ad-hoc tactics for model optimization, property decomposition and induction. In our work, we address the state-space explosion problem by using the architectural decomposition to partition the verification task for safety properties between AGREE tool and Simulink Design Verifier.

The SPEEDS approach to embedded system development [35] envisions rapid innovations through a model-based engineering paradigm supported by formal analyses. At its core, it requires that the architectural description of the system is annotated with assume-guarantee style contracts on components that cover both functional and non-functional aspects. Our present work can be seen as a key enabler for realizing the benefits of such an approach in the development of cyber-physical systems.

The BLESS annex and tool [20] supports reasoning over component-level behaviors defined using state machines and a simple imperative language. It supports component invariants and a variety of well-formedness properties for component behavior models. Unlike AGREE, which is fully automated, BLESS uses a user-driven deductive approach to proof. This allows specification of and reasoning about a larger class of properties, such as those involving non-linear arithmetic, than is currently supported with AGREE. On the other hand, BLESS specifications are defined on individual subcomponents and threads; there does not appear to be a notion of n-level composition of proof results across threads and systems.

8. CONCLUSION

We have presented a scalable and practical approach to compositionally verify a realistic medical cyber-physical system using commonly used modeling notations and readily available tools. Our assume-guarantee framework allows one to formally establish invariants of the full system by leveraging its hierarchical architectural decomposition for verification. This also allows the effective utilization of formal verification tools at the component-level, which may not be otherwise practical for verifying system-level properties. The partitioning of verification tasks along architectural lines has other benefits for system development: it provides early feedback on key architectural decisions, promotes iterative exploration of the solution space and fosters a synergistic evolution of requirements specification and system design. While there are some limitations in the kinds of models and properties that can be handled given our present choices of specification formalisms and verification techniques, we believe our approach represents a good trade-off point between the possible and the practical.

9. ACKNOWLEDGEMENTS

We would like to thank Andrew Gacek and Darren Cofer at Rockwell Collins for their insight and assistance in structuring and debugging the architectural models, and for developing JKind and AGREE.

10. REFERENCES

[1] Generic infusion pump project, http://rtg.cis.upenn.edu/gip.php3.

[2] A. Basu, S. Bensalem, M. Bozga, J. Combaz, M. Jaber, T.-H. Nguyen, and J. Sifakis. Rigorous component-based system design using the BIP framework. *Software, IEEE*, 28(3):41–48, 2011.

[3] E. Clarke, D. Long, and K. L. McMillan. Compositional model checking. In *Logic in Computer Science, 1989. LICS '89, Proceedings., Fourth Annual Symposium on*, pages 353–362, 1989.

[4] J. M. Cobleigh, G. S. Avrunin, and L. A. Clarke. Breaking up is hard to do: an investigation of decomposition for assume-guarantee reasoning. In *Proceedings of the 2006 international symposium on Software testing and analysis*, ISSTA '06, pages 97–108, New York, NY, USA, 2006. ACM.

[5] D. D. Cofer, A. Gacek, S. P. Miller, M. W. Whalen, B. LaValley, and L. Sha. Compositional verification of architectural models. In A. E. Goodloe and S. Person, editors, *Proceedings of the 4th NASA Formal Methods Symposium (NFM 2012)*, volume 7226, pages 126–140, Berlin, Heidelberg, April 2012. Springer-Verlag.

[6] L. de Alfaro and T. A. Henzinger. Interface automata. *SIGSOFT Softw. Eng. Notes*, 26(5):109–120, Sept. 2001.

[7] J.-F. Etienne, S. Fechter, and E. Juppeaux. Using simulink design verifier for proving behavioral properties on a complex safety critical system in the ground transportation domain. In M. Aiguier, F. Bretaudeau, and D. Krob, editors, *Complex Systems Design & Management*, pages 61–72. Springer Berlin Heidelberg, 2010.

[8] H. Ganzinger, G. Hagen, R. Nieuwenhuis, A. Oliveras, and C. Tinelli. DPLL(T): Fast decision procedures. In R. Alur and D. Peled, editors, *Proceedings of the 16th International Conference on Computer Aided Verification, CAV'04 (Boston, Massachusetts)*, volume 3114 of *Lecture Notes in Computer Science*, pages 175–188. Springer, 2004.

[9] O. Grumberg and D.E.Long. Model checking and modular verification. *ACM Transactions on Programming Languages and Systems*, 16(3):843–871, May 1994.

[10] G. Hagen and C. Tinelli. Scaling up the formal verification of lustre programs with smt-based techniques. In *Formal Methods in Computer-Aided Design, 2008. FMCAD '08*, pages 1–9, 2008.

[11] N. Halbwachs, P. Caspi, P. Raymond, and D. Pilaud. The synchronous data flow programming language LUSTRE. *Proceedings of the IEEE*, 79(9):1305–1320, 1991.

[12] A. Hall. Seven myths of formal methods. *IEEE Software*, September 1990.

[13] J. Hammond, R. Rawlings, and A. Hall. Will it work? [requirements engineering]. In *Requirements Engineering, 2001. Proceedings. Fifth IEEE International Symposium on*, pages 102 –109, 2001.

[14] D. Harel. Statecharts: A visual formalism for complex systems. *Science of Computer Programming*, 8(3):231–274, June 1987.

[15] D. Harel, R. Lampert, A. Marron, and G. Weiss. Model-checking behavioral programs. In *Proceedings of the ninth ACM international conference on Embedded software*, EMSOFT '11, pages 279–288, New York, NY, USA, 2011. ACM.

[16] IEEE. *IEEE Std. 1850-2005. Property Specification Language (PSL)*. IEEE, 2005.

[17] M. Jackson and P. Zave. Deriving specifications from requirements: An example. In *Proceedings of the Seventeenth International Conference on Software Engineering (ICSE'95)*, pages 15–24, May 1995.

[18] C. B. Jones. Tentative steps toward a development method for interfering programs. *ACM Trans. Program. Lang. Syst.*, 5(4):596–619, Oct. 1983.

[19] J. A. W. Kamp. *Tense Logic and the Theory of Linear Order*. PhD thesis, UCLA, 1968.

[20] B. Larson, P. Chalin, and J. Hatcliff. BLESS: Formal specification and verification of behaviors for embedded systems with software. In *Proceedings of the 5th NASA Formal Methods Symposium*. Springer-Verlag, 2013.

[21] N. A. Lynch and M. R. Tuttle. Hierarchical correctness proofs for distributed algorithms. In *Proceedings of the sixth annual ACM Symposium on Principles of distributed computing*, PODC '87, pages 137–151, New York, NY, USA, 1987. ACM.

[22] MathWorks. The MathWorks Inc. corporate web page. Via the world-wide-web: http://www.mathworks.com, 2004.

[23] Mathworks Inc. Simulink Design Verifier product web site. http://www.mathworks.com/products/sldesignverifier/.

[24] Mathworks Inc. Simulink product web site. http://www.mathworks.com/products/simulink.

[25] Mathworks Inc. Stateflow product web site. http://www.mathworks.com.

[26] K. McMillan. A methodology for hardware verification using compositional model checking. *Science of Computer Programming*, 37(1Ŭ3):279 – 309, 2000.

[27] K. L. McMillan. Circular compositional reasoning about liveness. Technical Report 1999-02, Cadence Berkeley Labs, Berkeley, CA 94704, 1999.

[28] S. P. Miller, A. C. Tribble, M. W. Whalen, and M. P. E. Heimdahl. Proving the shalls: Early validation of requirements through formal methods. *Int. J. Softw. Tools Technol. Transf.*, 8(4):303–319, 2006.

[29] J. Misra and K. Chandy. Proofs of networks of processes. *Software Engineering, IEEE Transactions on*, SE-7(4):417–426, 1981.

[30] A. Murugesan, S. Rayadurgam, and M. Heimdahl. Modes, features, and state-based modeling for clarity and flexibility. In *Fifth International Workshop on Modeling in Software Engineering*, May 2013.

[31] B. Nuseibeh. Weaving together requirements and architectures. *Computer*, 34:115–117, 2001.

[32] A. Pnueli. In transition from global to modular temporal reasoning about programs. In K. Apt, editor, *Logics and Models of Concurrent Systems*, volume 13 of *NATO ASI Series*, pages 123–144. Springer Berlin Heidelberg, 1985.

[33] SAE-AS5506. *Architecture Analysis and Design Language*. SAE, Nov 2004.

[34] M. Sheeran, S. Singh, and G. Stålmarck. Checking safety properties using induction and a sat-solver. In *FMCAD*, pages 108–125, 2000.

[35] SPEculative and Exporatory Design in System engineering. http://www.speeds.eu.com/, 2006-2009.

[36] M. W. Whalen, A. Gacek, D. Cofer, A. Murugesan, M. P. Heimdahl, and S. Rayadurgam. Your what is my how: Iteration and hierarchy in system design. *Software, IEEE*, 30(2):54–60, 2013.

Illustrating the AADL Error Modeling Annex (v. 2) Using a Simple Safety-Critical Medical Device*

Brian Larson, John Hatcliff, Kim Fowler
Kansas State University
{brl,hatcliff,kimrfowler}@ksu.edu

Julien Delange
Carnegie Mellon Software Engineering Institute
jdelange@sei.cmu.edu

ABSTRACT

Developing and certifying safety-critical and highly reliable systems almost always includes significant emphasis on hazard analysis and risk assessment. There have been substantial improvements in automation and formalization of other aspects of critical system engineering including model-driven development, analysis of source code and models, and verification techniques. However, hazard analysis and risk assessment are still largely manual and informal activities, tool support is limited (which for both development and auditing, increases time and effort and reduces accuracy and correctness), and artifacts are not integrated with architectural descriptions, system interfaces, high-level behavioral descriptions or code.

The Error Model annex of the Architecture Analysis and Design Language (AADL) provides formal and automated support for a variety of forms of hazard analysis and risk assessment activities. Specifically, it enables engineers to formally specify errors, error propagation, error mitigation – using annotations that are integrated with formal architecture and behavioral descriptions written in AADL. Plug-ins to the Open-Source AADL Tool Environment (OSATE) process these annotations to provide various forms of (semi)-automated support for reliability predication and tasks necessary to support common hazard analysis and risk assessment techniques such as Failure Modes and Effects Analysis (FMEA), Fault Tree Analysis (FTA), and Functional Hazard Analysis (FHA).

In this paper, we illustrate basic aspects of Error Modeling in AADL using a simple safety-critical medical system – an infant incubator called "Isolette". We summarize standard tasks involved in FMEA and FTA, we illustrate the principal steps involved in AADL Error Modeling for the Isolette, and we describe how those steps relate to FMEA and FTA.

We give a brief survey of emerging automated analysis tools implemented as plug-ins to the AADL OSATE environment that process error modeling annotations. We believe this introduction to Error Modeling in AADL can expose engineers of high-integrity systems to techniques and tools that can provide a more rigorous, automated, and integrated approach to important risk management activities.

Categories and Subject Descriptors

D.2.4 [**Software Engineering**]: Software/Program Verification—*Formal Methods, Reliability*; D.2.6 [**Programming Environments**]: [Integrated environments]; D.2.11 [**Software Architectures**]: [Languages]

Keywords

hazard analysis, risk assessment, error modeling, error analysis, AADL, formal architecture

1. INTRODUCTION

Innovations in model-driven development, static analyses, type systems, and automated deduction techniques have improved methods and tools for developing high-integrity systems. These improvements center around system design, implementation, and verification and validation. However, developing and certifying safety-critical and highly reliable systems includes additional activities such as hazard analysis techniques (HAT), risk assessment, and reliability predictions that play an important role in safety evaluation and certification [4, 13].[1] For example, "bottom up" hazard analysis techniques assess how individual components of a system may fail and analyze (via a systematic tracing of system data and control paths as well as other more indirect notions of coupling) how those failures might impact the desired functionality and safety of the system. "Top down" techniques may start by identifying (a) the forms of accidents and losses that should be avoided, and (b) system states that might lead to those accidents, and then proceed by tracing down through the system architecture, design, or implementation to identify failures or faults that might lead to those

*Work supported in part by the US National Science Foundation (NSF) (#0932289, #1239543), the NSF US Food and Drug Administration Scholar-in-Residence Program (#1065887, #1238431) the National Institutes of Health / NIBIB Quantum Program, and the US Air Force Office of Scientific Research (AFOSR) (#FA9550-09-1-0138).

[1] According to Leveson [14, pp. 7–14], and we agree, safety is not synonymous with reliability. Safety is freedom from accidents – events that result in loss of life or some other form of loss important to system stakeholders. Reliability is the probability that a piece of equipment or component will perform its intended function satisfactorily for a prescribed time and under stipulated environment conditions. The techniques and tools that we discuss in this paper can address both safety and reliability.

states. Tooling and automated support for these safety and risk assessment activities has not kept pace with advances in other dimensions of development highlighted above.

1.1 Short-comings in Conventional Risk Assessment Techniques

Informal (non-machine readable) inputs: Advances in software development environments have illustrated the usefulness of attaching various forms of annotations and pragmas directly in source code and other machine-readable development artifacts. These annotations and artifacts into which they are embedded can then be used as inputs to automated analyses that propagate information through artifacts and either produce additional annotations or analysis results directly linked to the artifacts. For example, in modern development environments for Java, C#, and Ada, a developer may introduce simple annotations indicating that certain variables are intended to hold reference values that are *always non-null* (remaining variables are allowed to hold either null *or* non-null values). This information is then propagated throughout the program to (a) deduce when other variables are always non-null and (b) to detect possible run-time exceptions due to dereference of null pointers.

Unfortunately, despite long-standing formal approaches from academia [8] and automation in some commercial tools, inputs to HAT are most commonly captured in separate natural-language-based text documents or spreadsheets. Thus, even though many aspects of HAT include identifying component failure modes (which, *e.g.*, could be captured as simple enumeration annotations attached to a component) and reasoning about propagation of information (*e.g.*, how faults and effects of faults flow through the system), the primary inputs to HAT (*e.g.*, system architectures including both hardware and software component structures, component failure rates, common hazards for a particular device type) are usually not represented formally or precisely enough for now-common paradigms of code-level static flow analysis and extended type-checking to be applied in support of HAT.

Manual construction: One of the main purposes of HAT is to systematically guide engineers through a set of analysis steps leading to critical decision points – points in the analysis that require judgements about the absence or presence of hazards, risk mitigation strategies, and the degree of residual risk. However, many of the steps leading up to these decision points are highly repetitive and intermediate results are calculated in a straightforward manner from other development artifacts (*e.g.*, identifying enclosing components or subsystems in a Failure Modes and Effects Analysis (FMEA)). Although some tools exist provide limited forms of automated support for these steps, such tools are not widely applied and their effectiveness is limited. The practical impact is that the bulk of HAT activities are carried out manually.

Lack of integration with development artifacts and limited traceability: In current practice, activities and results of HAT are recorded in text editors or spreadsheets. Information driving HAT, including specifications of system architecture descriptions, dependencies between system components, and inter-component information flow is spread across many artifacts. This hinders traceability between different artifacts, and the informal nature of the information representation prevents automated support for navigating traceability links. In contrast, an approach that includes for-

mal descriptions of system architectures could enable HAT information including error types, error propagation paths, and component failure probabilities to be captured directly as annotations in a system architecture description.

1.2 AADL and Error Modeling Annex

AADL [6, 1] is a strong candidate for formal architecture specification in high-integrity systems. AADL was created in response to the high cost associated with (far too frequent) failed subsystem integration attempts due to ambiguous or incompletely documented component interfaces. AADL is now used in several industrial development settings. For example, on the System Architecture Virtual Integration (SAVI) effort, aircraft manufacturers together with subcontractors use AADL to define a precise system architecture using an "integrate then build" design approach. In this approach, important interactions are specified, interfaces are designed, and integration is verified before the internals of components are built. Once correct integration is established, contractors provide implementations that are compliant with the architecture [7, 19].

A number of AADL users are interested in the development of hazard analysis, reliability prediction, and risk assessment techniques (all separate but related issues) that can be deeply integrated with formal architecture specifications and system integration activities. This interest has prompted the development of the AADL Error Modeling framework. AADL includes an *annex* mechanism by which additional modeling notations or supporting tools can be added to the standard, and this mechanism is used to define the current version of the Error Modeling Framework – Error Model Version 2 (EMV2). As described in the EMV2 annex document [5], EMV2 enables modeling of different types of faults, fault behavior of individual system components, modeling of fault propagation affecting related components in terms of peer to peer interactions and deployment relationships between software components and their execution platform, modeling of aggregation of fault behavior and propagation in terms of the component hierarchy, as well as specification of fault tolerance strategies expected in the actual system architecture. The objective of EMV2 is to support qualitative and quantitative assessments of system dependability, *i.e.*, reliability, availability, integrity (safety, security), and survivability, as well as compliance of the system to the specified fault tolerance strategies from an annotated architecture model of the embedded software, computer platform, and physical system. Thus, EMV2 provides a foundation for addressing the shortcomings described in Section 1.1.

1.3 This Paper

We have found it useful to advocate for the use of AADL EMV2 by illustrating its application to simple systems and by explicitly identifying how it might support and improve upon aspects of conventional risk assessment techniques. Regarding the shortcomings of conventional risk assessment techniques identified above, AADL EMV2 provides formal machine-readable inputs to the risk assessment process that are directly integrated with formal architecture descriptions and other implementation oriented artifacts. This provides an annotation-based approach to HAT that developers will recognize as similar to annotation-based code-level static analysis and verification techniques. With these formal architecture-integrated annotations as a foundation, we believe that many of the tedious, repetitive, and error prone, manual steps in HAT can be automated. Moreover, because the vision of AADL includes code generation from formal architecture descriptions, the architecture-integrated approach of EMV2 provides the basis for eventual development of risk assessment tools that offer strong traceability throughout implementation-oriented development artifacts.

The specific contributions of this paper are as follows:

- We illustrate the basic error modeling constructs and methodology of AADL EMV2 using a simple safety-critical system – an infant incubator, referred to as an "Isolette." This example, orginally introduced by Lempia and Miller in the FAA Requirements Engineering Management Handbook [12], is also being used by Blouin to illustrate the AADL Requirements Annex [3]. Thus, the work in this paper contributes to what we hope will eventually be an end-to-end illustration of AADL-based development using the Isolette example.
- We describe how EMV2 modeling and tools formalize and provide automated support for important artifacts and tasks required in conventional risk assessment techniques including FMEA and FTA.
- We provide as open-source artifacts the AADL models for the Isolette including EMV2 annotations.[2]

2. ISOLETTE EXAMPLE

The Federal Aviation Administration's (FAA) Requirements Engineering Management Handbook (REMH) [12] uses an example of an infant incubator called an "Isolette" to illustrate best practices for writing requirements for embedded systems. We use the Isolette as the primary illustration in this paper because it is relatively simple (and thus can be discussed within the space constraints of this paper) while still rich enough to illustrate a number of dimensions in risk assessment.

Figure 1 presents a diagram the Isolette's primary system components and environment interactions. The Isolette thermostat takes as input an air temperature value from a temperature sensor and controls a heat sources to produce an air temperature within a target range specified by the clinician through the operator interface. Safety concerns include ensuring that infant is not harmed by air temperature inside the isolette being too hot or too cool. The Isolette uses a subsystem separate from the operational thermostat to sound an alarm if hazardous temperatures are detected.

Figure 2 illustrates the AADL graphical component architecture notation for the top-level system architecture for the Isolette. Triangles represent component ports, and lines represent data flow connections between ports. AADL also includes a textual representation that allows a variety of formal specification and property notations to be associated with different elements in the architecture. Space constraints do not permit a detailed explanation, but important AADL features are rich structuring support (allowing nested components, grouping of ports and connections, abstract components and refinement, etc.), buffered and unbuffered ports, a variety of dispatch modes for threads (event triggered, time triggered), as well as a rich type system and a

---

[2]The Isolette AADL+EMV2 artifacts are available at http://santos.cis.ksu.edu/BLESS/examples/isolette.zip.

rigorous notion of what it means for two opposing ports to be "plug-compatible."

3. CONVENTIONAL RISK ASSESSMENT TECHNIQUES

3.1 Failure Modes and Effects Analysis (FMEA)

Failure Modes and Effects Analysis (FMEA), helps a designer to determine if the design must change or improve to reduce potential failures. FMEA examines single-point failures, both their types and propagation to systemic effects. FMEA has the primary purpose of determining operational faults and safety. FMEA can have the secondary purpose of estimating the system reliability from the component reliabilities [4, pp. 235–259]. FMEA is a tabular, bottom-up approach for single-point failures; it is both qualitative and quantitative in nature. It helps a designer or analyst to determine failure effects at various levels: functional or component level, modular or assembly level, subsystem level, and top-level system.

Typically a designer or analyst will begin the FMEA at a specific level of abstraction in an architecture, consider the component boundaries (interfaces) at the level of abstraction, and study how failures propagate and affect other subsystems [4, pp. 235–259]. The goal for FMEA is to assess system functionality and safety in the event that a component fails. FMEA aims to identify both the type of failure within each component and its effect on component behavior. Once identified and the component and system effects understood, FMEA aims to determine the extent of criticality for the system. The criticality helps a developer to address risks in reliability and to set priorities during design. An FMEA, which can occupy hundreds of pages and is often manually prepared by a domain expert, can tell a regulator that the designer(s) attempted a measure of discipline and rigor during development. While quantity does not imply discipline and rigor, it can be an indicator of effort. The point is that performing FMEA correctly is a lot of work; automation and integrated tools such as those offered by the OSATE EMV2 tools are sorely needed.

FMEA attempts to answer these questions:

- How can each component fail?
- What are the effects of each failure?
- What are the consequences of each failure?

The effects are the physical manifestations of a failure. The consequences are the outworking of those manifestations on the system or its operators.

If reliability data are available, then FMEA addresses these questions as well:

- How frequently can a component fail?
- How does a component's failure affect system reliability?

3.1.1 FMEA Inputs

Part 1: Determine the system context, its mission, system design, the level of analysis (component, module, or subsystem), operational constraints (e.g. logical dependencies, data flow), and the boundaries where failures appear or stop. Failure effects propagate over boundaries or are contained by them.

Part 2: Determine specific data for each component:

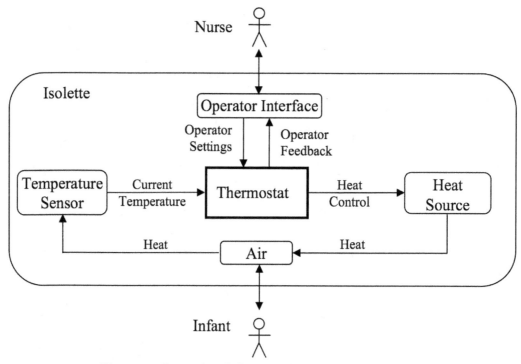

Figure 1: Operational Context for Isolette Thermostat

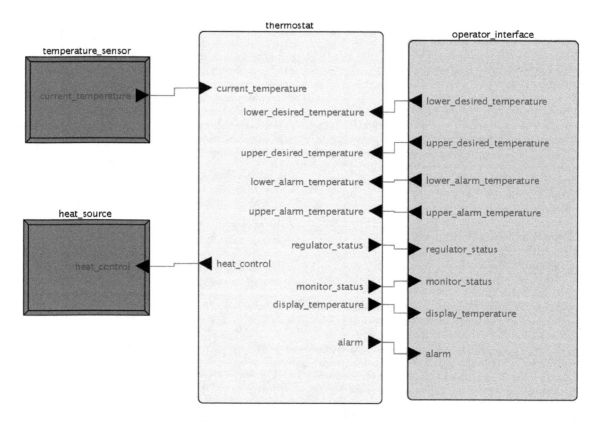

Figure 2: AADL Model of Isolette

- Possible failure types, e.g. two electrical signal pins shorted together
- Possible operational modes, e.g. expected mechanical actions from control operations
- Connection to other components
- Immediate effects of failure
- Systemic effects of failure
- (For reliability calculations: probability of failure or occurrence)

3.1.2 FMEA Outputs

The results of a FMEA are typically listed in tabular form and include, for each component, an enumeration of the modes in which a component can fail, the immediate effect of those failures as visible at the component's boundary, and the potential effects of the failure at the system level. Figure 3 illustrates just one set of potential failure effects for the heating element component of the Isolette.

3.1.3 FMEA Methodology / Tasks

Step 1: Understand and list potential hazards that lead to failures within the system. List the components to be analyzed.

Step 2: Collect and list failure modes for each component. An example of domain expertise, for the isolette, is that a designer might know that a heater element can experience corrosion in its connectors that increases electrical resistance and lowers heat dissipation.

Step 3: Collect and list effects for each component. The immediate effect is the failure as observed at component or module boundary, e.g. the module stops operating. The systemic effect is the observed effect of failure on overall system behavior, e.g. a failed module forces the system to stop operating. Note that examining more failure effects multiplies the number of lines in the analysis; also moving towards the component level and greater detail greatly expands the effort in developing FMEA.

Step 4: (if calculating reliability) - List probability of failure for each component (*e.g.*, from MIL-HDBK-217). This step assumes independent failures, that is there are no common causes between component failures.

Step 5: (if warranted or desired) - additional columns can be added to enhance understanding of failures and hazards as suggested by Ericson [4, pp. 235–259]:

- Causal factors between failure mode and effects columns to give more comment to type or location of failure or extenuating circumstances
- Method of failure detection after the effects columns, e.g.: inspection, test, none
- controls after the failure detection column, *e.g.*, Quality Assurance (QA), Built-in-test, None
- Hazard after the controls column, *e.g.*, Fire, Premature operation, Damage, None
- Final column for "Recommended Action"

3.2 Fault Tree Analysis (FTA)

Fault Tree Analysis, or FTA, helps a designer to determine if the design must change or improve to reduce potential failures. FTA examines sources, or root causes, of potential faults; it starts with descriptions of high-level, systemic fault types and then traces down to lower-level subsystems and modules to potential explanatory causes. FTA has the primary purpose of educating designers to potential problems for operational faults and safety. FTA has the secondary purpose of performing root cause analysis when a fault occurs [4, pp. 183–221].

FTA is a graphical, top-down approach for examining high-level faults. FTA is both qualitative and quantitative; it uses Boolean algebra, logic, and probability to generate descriptions of fault paths from cause to systemic effect. Like FMEA, FTA helps a designer or analyst to determine failure effects at various levels: functional or component level, modular or assembly level, subsystem level, and top-level system. Unlike FMEA, FTA can handle multiple, simultaneous failures and can support probabilistic risk assessment [4, pp. 183–221].

The goal for FTA is a top-down analysis focused on system design. FTA aims to identify potential root causes of system-level faults, which can provide a basis for reducing safety risks and can document safety considerations. Once FTA identifies potential root causes, the designer can assign criticality of the fault for the system. Like FMEA, assigning criticality within FTA helps a developer to address risks in safety (or reliability if reliability calculations are included) and set priorities during design. An FTA, which can occupy hundreds of pages and is often manually prepared by a domain expert, can tell a regulator that the designer(s) attempted a measure of discipline and rigor during development. As with FMEA, the same caveats regarding quality and quantity apply, and improvements in tooling and automation would provide significant benefits.

FTA attempts to answer these questions:

- What are the root causes of failures?
- What are the combinations and probabilities of causal factors in undesired events?
- What are the mechanisms and fault paths of undesired events?

FTA is similar to FMEA in using criticality and reliability but from a top-down perspective that can handle multiple, simultaneous failures. If criticality data are included, then FTA can address risk to reduce both severity and likelihood of problems. If reliability data are available, can calculate the probability of failure.

3.2.1 FTA Methodology / Tasks

Step 1: Define the system by collecting design artifacts, such as requirements, schematics, source code, and models. Layout the concept of operations, or CONOPs, to further the definition. Finally, understand the system behavior.

Step 2: Define undesired fault event by performing the following:

- Identify the final outcome of the undesired event
- Identify sub-events that lead to final event
- Begin to structure the connections using logic-gates
- Do Step 3 before completing structure of connections

Step 3: Establish rules of analysis by defining the boundaries of the analysis and the concepts that you can use: [4, pp. 194].

- I-N-S, which means, What is immediate (I), necessary (N), and sufficient (S) to cause the event? I-N-S helps the analyst from jumping ahead and focus on event chain.

Com-ponent	Failure	Immediate effect	System effect	failure rate (failures/yr.)	probability of detection	
Heater element	fails open	airflow not heated	patient not warmed, alarm will sound once temperature drops below threshold, display will show low temperature	0.0876	0.9999	
	fails on	airflow continuously heated, thermosafety switch opens on high temperature turning off heater	patient warmed too much, alarm will sound once temperature raises above threshold, display will show high temperature	1.9E-05	0.999	
	fails to heat to specification	airflow not heated completely but warm enough	patient warmed sufficiently, display shows correct temperature	0.00028	0.05	
	fails to heat to specification	airflow not heated completely and not warm enough for application	patient not warmed, alarm will sound once temperature drops below threshold, display will show low temperature	0.0876	0.9	
	fails intermittent	airflow heated sometimes, not other times	when failure is open then patient not warmed, alarm will sound once temperature drops below threshold, display will show low temperature	0.0876	0.9	
	fails intermittent	airflow heated sometimes, not other times	When heater is operational then patient warmed sufficiently, display shows correct temperature	6.6E-05	0.8	

Figure 3: Example FMEA Outputs for Isolette (excerpts)

- SS-SC, asks, What is the source of the fault?
    - If the fault is a component failure, then classify as SC (state-of-the-component) fault.
    - If the fault is not component failure, then classify as SS (state-of-the-system) fault.
    - If the fault is SC, then perform event ORs of the P-S-C inputs.
    - If the fault is SS, then develop the event further by using I-N-S logic.
- P-S-C, which means, "What are the primary (P), secondary (S), and command (C) causes of the event?" P-S-C helps the analyst focus on specific causal factors.

Step 4: Build the fault tree, which is a repetitive process. At each level determine the cause, the effect, and the logical combination of logic symbols. The construction rules are almost self-evident but Ericson describes good, disciplined techniques [4, pp. 195–197].

Step 5: Establish cut sets, which are critical path(s) of subevent combinations that cause the undesirable final state event. While Ericson provides in-depth mathematical treatment of cut sets and probabilities, you can often perform a mere inspection to reveal the weak links that indicate the most important cut set(s) that lead to the fault event [4, pp. 199–206].

3.2.2 FTA Outputs

Figure 4 provides excerpts of an FTA report for the Isolette. This example output illustrates potential root causes for a failure to warm the air in the Isolette. Use of the top level OR-gate indicates that the failure may have several causes including an operator error, heater subsystem failure, air flow blockage, or thermosafety switch failure.

4. ERROR MODELING WITH AADL

The capability to model fault behavior, and from that model predict failure rates, was integral to MetaH from which AADL was derived. The original AADL standard SAE AS5506 incorporated some basic error modeling capabilities. The SAE International standard subcommittee AS-2C is expected put to ballot in the summer of 2013 a substantial revision to the error model framework, designated as Error Model Version 2 (EMV2). EMV2 incorporates several improvements such as a flexible error type system and pre-declared error type hierarchies with formal semantics.

As described in the AADL EMV2 draft standard [5, Section E.1], from the bottom-up, the error models of low-level components typically capture the results of failure modes and effects analysis. From the top-down, the error models of the overall system and high-level subsystems typically capture the results of system hazard analysis. One purpose of the formal modeling approach enabled by EMV2 is to ensure that the results of these analyses as captured in an architecture specification are consistent and complete with respect to each other. This enables an integrated approach that insures consistency and completeness between hazard analysis, failure modes and effects analysis (FMEA), and the safety and reliability analyses that relate the two.

In this section, we give an example-driven introduction to the basic EMV2 language constructs. While we aim for a reasonable coverage of constructs, space constraints do not permit a discussion of some of the more advanced features. We hope to provide a broader discussion in an expanded version of this paper to be released in the near future.

4.1 Faults, Errors, and Failures

Unfortunately, there are varying definitions in the literature of common terms such as faults, errors, and failures. To ground our discussions in upcoming sections, we present below definitions used in the EMV2 annex document [5].

A *fault* is a root (phenomenological) cause of an error that can potentially result in a failure, i.e., an anomalous undesired change in the structure or data within a component that may cause that component to eventually fail to perform according to its nominal specification, i.e., result in malfunction or loss of function. Examples of faults include overheating of hardware circuits, or programmers making coding mistakes when producing source text. Errors, resulting failures, and error propagations are effects of a fault. The activation of a fault is represented by the Error Model concept of *error event*.

An *error* is the difference in state from a correct state. The activation of a fault places a compo-

70

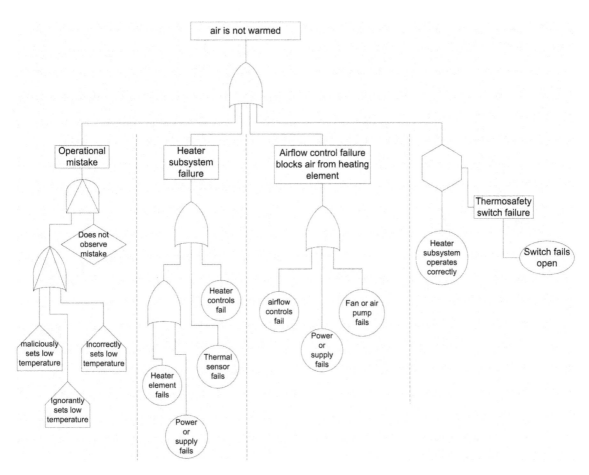

Figure 4: Example FTA Outputs for Isolette (excerpts)

nent into such an error state (possibly after some delay). An erroneous component may persist in that error state for some period of time before it behaves in a way that violates its nominal specification. For example, a burned out transistor (an activated fault) in an adder circuit does not cause a processor to violate its nominal specification until that circuit is used (after a delay) and produces an incorrect output value (erroneous state information). The Error Model concept of *error behavior state machine* is used to define error states, transitions, and conditions that trigger a transition.

A *failure* is a deviation in behavior from a nominal specification, i.e., a component can no longer function as intended in terms malfunction and loss of function as a consequence of an error. This may be due to an activated fault within the component or an error propagation from another component. The deviation can be characterized by type, persistence, and degree of severity. The degree to which a failure affects nominal behavior is referred to as severity of the failure. The Error Model concept of *error type* associated with error events, error states, and error propagations, as well as properties are used to characterize a failure.

4.2 Error Types

Hazard analysis techniques such as FMEA, Fault Hazard Analysis, and Subsystem Hazard Analysis [4] often include reasoning about (a) the different ways in which a component may fail and (b) how faults in one component can impact other components in a system.

EMV2 provides the ability to declare *error types* that represents a categorization or taxonomy of faults and errors relevant for a system. The error model language for the first version of AADL (AS5506) (which we refer to as EMV1) modeled only one kind of error. Users did all sorts of creative things with names to represent kinds of errors or faults. Nevertheless, Aerospace Corporation used EMV1 to model errors in satellites and ground stations with *thousands* of AADL components from which Markov models were extracted and solved. The enhancements included in EMV2 were inspired by the Fault Propagation and Transformation Calculus (FPTC)[18], developed by Wallace at York University. EMV2 improves upon FPTC by adding an error type system with elegant ways of expressing groups and combinations of errors.[3]

In EMV2, an error type can represent a category of fault arising in a certain component, the category of error being propagated, or the category of error represented by the error behavior state of a system or component. Error types can be organized into different type hierarchies, e.g., types relating to value errors and types relating to timing errors. These type hierarchies give rise to the conventional subtyping/inclusion polymorphism found in object-oriented languages with inheritance.

---

[3]The first author has been made significant contributions to the error type system of EMV2, including simplifying the original proposal for EMV2's type system, refactoring the EMV2 grammar to reduce the number of productions by two-thirds, and proposing a cleaner semantics.

Figure 5 gives a conceptual view of common error types that are *pre-defined* in EMV2. The left side of the figure illustrates errors related to the function of system services. For example, in the context of network enabled applications, the failure of the system to initialize its network authentication service might be classified as a *Service Omission* error. The right side of the figure illustrates errors that might be associated with data values or the communication of those values. Regarding the timing errors on the far right side of the figure, the failure of a network or bus to deliver a data value from a provider to a client within the bounds of its quality of service contract might be classified as a *Late Delivery Error*. In the value errors, a component that emits on its interface a value that lies outside of its specified range might be classified as an `OutOfRange` error. As an example of the subtyping that arises from such hierarchies, an `OutOfRange` error can be either an `AboveRange` error or an `BelowRange` error.

Error hierarchies such as those graphically represented in Figure 5, are actually defined textually in an AADL annex clause. Figure 6 provides an excerpt of the textual representation corresponding to the error types presented on the right-hand side of Figure 5.

```
TimingError: type;
EarlyDelivery: type extends TimingError;
LateDelivery: type extends TimingError;
ValueError: type;
UndetectableValueError: type extends
  ValueError;
BenignValueError: type extends ValueError;
OutOfRange: type extends BenignValueError;
OutOfBounds: type extends BenignValueError;
BelowRange: type extends OutOfRange;
AboveRange: type extends OutOfRange;
```

Figure 6: Standard, Predeclared Timing and Value Error Type Declarations

EMV2 also provides the ability to declare error types customized to a particular application. These may be completely new hierarchies, or they may extend or rename predefined error types. As presented in Section 3.1.3 **Step 2**, initial steps in a FMEA will identify failure modes for each component. For the Isolette example, we might use an EMV2 custom error definition like the one in Figure 7 to capture basic failure modes and other errors related to analysis of the Isolette. Hierarchy is used to introduce categories for `Alarm` and `Status` errors. These are subsequently refined to errors for specific Isolette components. The declaration of `ThreadFault` illustrates the ability to rename an EMV2 predeclared error type to obtain an Isolette-relevant name.

A heat-control error may harm the infant by becoming too hot or cold. Therefore, `HeatControlError` is the most important error type. The hazard for this error is mitigated by sounding an alarm if the isolette becomes dangerously warm or cool.

4.3 Attaching Error Sources to Architectural Models

In conventional approaches to HAT, association of different errors to system components and behaviors is only done *informally* in textual documentation – making the informa-

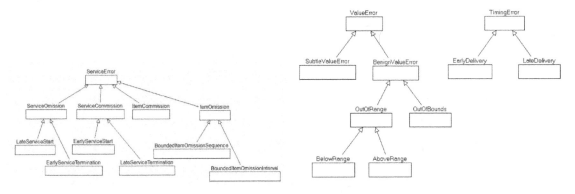

Figure 5: AADL Predeclared Error Types (excerpts)

```
annex EMV2
{**
error types
  HeatControlError: type;
  AlarmError : type;
  FalseAlarm : type extends AlarmError;
  MissedAlarm : type extends AlarmError;
  StatusError : type;
  RegulatorStatusError : type extends
    StatusError;
  RegulatorModeError : type extends
    StatusError;
  MonitorStatusError : type extends
    StatusError;
  MonitorModeError : type extends
    StatusError;
  ThreadFault renames type
    ErrorLibrary::EarlyServiceTermination;
  InternalError : type;
  DetectedFault : type;
  UndetectedFault : type;
end types;
**};
```

Figure 7: Custom Isolette Error Types

```
device temperature_sensor_ts features
  current_temperature : out data port
    Iso_Variables::current_temperature;
annex EMV2
{**
error propagations
  use types ErrorLibrary;
  current_temperature: out propagation
    {OutOfRange,UndetectableValueError};
flows  --define source of errors
  f: error source current_temperature
    {OutOfRange,UndetectableValueError};
properties
  EMV2::Occurrence =>  --out-of-range likelihood
    Iso_Properties::TemperatureSensorOutOfRange
      applies to current_temperature.OutOfRange;
  EMV2::Occurrence =>  --undetectable likelihood
    Iso_Properties::SensorUndetectableValueError
      applies to
        current_temperature.UndetectableValueError;
end propagations;
**};
end temperature_sensor_ts;
```

Figure 8: Temperature Sensor Error Model

tion hard to leverage in automated analysis or automated traceability queries. For example, as illustrated in Figure 3 of Section 3.1.2, in a conventional FMEA, the analysis would involve creating a table in a text document (perhaps following some template) that associates a component with the particular faults that occur within it. By formalizing both architecture and error types in AADL and EMV2, one can *formally* associate an error with a component by directly annotating the architecture model. With this information in place, not only can (all or portions of) conventional textual reports like those in Figure 3 be auto-generated, but the information can also be leveraged for automated analysis.

As an example, Figure 8 captures error properties of the temperature sensor component of the Isolette (see Figure 2). We aim to capture the fact that faults within the temperature sensor may cause it to produce both (a) erroneous temperatures that can be detected because the values are outside of the specified range of the sensor, or (b) temperatures that are within range (and thus cannot be detected by a range check), but are nevertheless incorrect. To formalize the results of Section 3.1.3 **Step 3** in which one identifies the immediate effects of a component failure as observed at

component or module boundary, we begin by declaring that data emitted from port `current_temperature` may have error types `OutOfRange` and `UndetectableValueError` (*i.e.*, in range, but incorrect). The flow declaration indicates that this component is the *source* of the error, *i.e.*, the error originates internally to the component and does not flow into the component from the context, and that the error may impact other components in the context via the `current_temperature` output port. To formalize the reliability information called out in Section 3.1.3 **Step 4**, the occurrence properties provide information concerning the probability of occurrence for each of the errors, which can be leveraged by a variety of probabilistic analyses. For hardware components, such probabilities might be derived from MIL-HDBK-217F *Reliability Prediction of Electronic Equipment* or similar sources.

4.4 Error Propagation, Termination, and Transformation

Common HAT, including FMEA, require as input the possible ways that one component could interact or interfere with another. The example FEMA output in Figure 3 of Section 3.1.2 illustrates that reports following the recommended

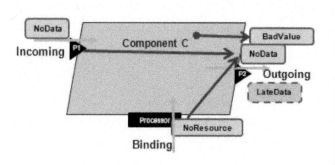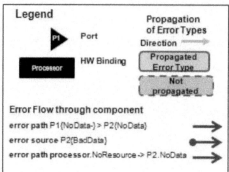

Figure 9: AADL EMV2 Error Propagation (from the AADL Error Model Annex)

```
system implementation isolette.impl
subcomponents
  thermostat : system thermostat_th.impl;
  temperature_sensor : device
    temperature_sensor_ts.impl;
  heat_source : device heat_source_hs.impl;
  operator_interface : system
    operator_interface_oi.impl;
connections
ct : port
  temperature_sensor.current_temperature
    -> thermostat.current_temperature;
  . . .
end isolette.impl;
```

Figure 10: AADL Isolette Component Implementation

```
  current_temperature : in data port
    Iso_Variables::current_temperature;
  . . .
annex EMV2 {**
  use types ErrorLibrary, isolette;
  error propagations
  current_temperature: in propagation
    {OutOfRange,UndetectableValueError};
  alarm: out propagation {AlarmError};
  monitor_status: out propagation
    {MonitorStatusError};
  regulator_failure: in propagation
    {ItemOmission,ItemComission};
  end propagations;
**};
end thermostat_th;
```

Figure 11: Thermostat declarations illustrating EMV2 error propagations

format for recording FMEA outputs often have large gaps in justification/reasoning about effects and impact of errors. In particular, the FEMA output lists immediate effects of a failure at the current component boundary and then lists systemic effects. Intuitively, to derive the systemic effect, one would need to reason about how errors propagate through the components in the system, *i.e.*, one would need to reason about error paths. Interactions between components giving rise to propagation paths could be either be intended and be explicit in the architecture (*e.g.*, port connections reflecting read/write relationships between components) or be unintended (*e.g.*, electrical arcing, or electromagnetic interference or heat damage due inadequate shielding). AADL EMV2 provides formal specification of both direct/explicit and indirect/implicit interactions. Thus, it provides a rigorous methodology and formal justification for how one can move from reasoning about the immediate effects of a failure to systemic effects. Here, we limit the discussion to how EMV2 captures explicit interactions.

Figure 9 (taken from from the AADL Error Model Annex specification) illustrates that EMV2 enables one to declare how errors flow along interaction points of components (*e.g.*, features such as ports as well as deployment bindings). For example, the `BadValue` error can originate within the component and propagate out the `P2` port. In contrast, the `NoData` originates in the component's context, flows into the `P1` port and is propagated through the component and out the `P2` port. One can also declare that the component should not produce a `LateValue` error; similar declarations capture the fact that an incoming error is recognized within the component and mitigated in some way. In general, for each component one can specify an error flow indicating whether a component is the source or sink of an error propagation (indicated by `source` and `sink` keywords), or whether it passes

on an incoming propagation as an outgoing propagation of the same or different error type (indicated by `path` keyword).

Components sometimes transform errors. A component detecting an out-of-range error on an incoming data port can transform it into an omission error (by discarding the data) rather than sending bad data to the next component. In this way, transmission, detection, suppression, and transformation can be modeled. For medical devices, precise characterization of error types and their flows allows risk analysis to focus on those error types that (may) cause patient harm.

Consider the example of explicit interaction (captured in our AADL formal architecture specification of Figure 10) over the connection `ct` that communicates temperature data between the temperature sensor and the thermostat. When reasoning about the fault/failure properties of the thermostat, we wish to indicate how errors coming from the thermostat's system context may propagate or be mitigated by the thermostat. In the EMV2 annotations in Figure 11, we indicate that the port `current_temperature` of the thermostat is prepared to receive propagations of error types `OutOfRange` and `UndetectableValueError`. If other error types such as `TimingError` could be received, the inconsistency will be identified by the EMV2 plugin to OSATE. This illustrates the similarity between error model analysis and error-type-checking in AADL models and conventional static analysis and type-checking on source code. Figure 11 also illustrates that *error type sets* allow multiple error types to be treated together. Error type sets are enclosed by curly brackets. The error types expected on in port `current_temperature` is the error type set `{OutOfRange,UndetectableValueError}`. Similarly, out port `monitor_status` emits the only error type in its set, `Moni-`

torStatusError. Note that the error type OutOfRange includes both AboveRange and BelowRange by inheritance.

Another structuring mechanism, *error products*, enables one to characterize an error in terms of a conjunction of error types. For example: a message may be late; a message may have incorrect value; a message may be both late and incorrect as captured by the respective error types below.
{LateDelivery, ValueError, LateDelivery*ValueError}

An error product (the star) defines a new error type to be the confluence of multiple error types.[4]

To illustrate situations in which errors are transformed, consider the interaction between the temperature sensor and heat source reflected in Figure 12. The declared error path indicates that an incoming UndetectableValueError on the current_temperature port becomes a HeatControlError on the heat_control output port because the bad temperature value was used to control the heat source.

```
flows mrmsve:
  error path current_temperature
    {UndetectableValueError} ->
      heat_control(HeatControlError);
```

Figure 12: Error Flow Path

4.5 Error State Machines

The manner in which a component generates or propagates errors often depends on the error state of components. For example, a completely failed component transmits no errors. EMV2 allows the definition of error state machines, and their association with components. In the Isolette example, a simple error state machine models this notion. When such a state machine is specified, the error propagation behavior of a component (omitted due to space constraints) may be conditioned on specific states in the state machine (see Figure 16).

It is important to understand that an error state machine is not an abstraction of a system's functional implementation; it does not specify, *e.g.*, the transition semantics of error handling routines. One would not generate implementation code from an error state machine. Rather, an error state machine is an analysis artifact that reflects the analyst's understanding of how a component generates and transforms error types in a manner that depends on the operational state of the component. Error state machines model the existence of errors that may not (yet) be detected.

4.5.1 Events

Error events trigger transitions of error state machines. Figure 13 shows the declaration of error event fail.

```
events fail: error event;
```

Figure 13: Error Event

4.5.2 States

Error states represent the current error behavior of its component. Exactly one error state must be initial.

----
[4]Error products are not used in the Isolette example, and are included here for completeness.

Figure 14 shows the declaration of two error states, working and failed, of which working is the initial state.

```
states
  working: initial state;
  failed : state;
```

Figure 14: Error States

4.5.3 Transitions

Error transitions define changes of error state, caused by an error event. Figure 15 says a fail event causes transition from working state to failed state.

```
transitions
  working -[fail]-> failed;
```

Figure 15: Error State Machine Transition

4.5.4 Three Error State Machines

The EMV2 annex library in isolette.aadl defines three state machines used by components. The simplest error state machine models components that stop when they fail. When component's EMV2 annex subclause includes "use behavior isolette::FailStop;", it means to use the state machine defined in Figure 16 to model its errors.

```
--error state machine for components that
--have out-of range values when failed
  error behavior FailStop
    use types isolette;
    events fail: error event;
    states
      working: initial state;
      failed : state;
    transitions
      working -[fail]-> failed;
end behavior;
```

Figure 16: Fail-Stop Error State Machine

The next error state machine is used to model components, that have become unreliable, but have not failed outright. The temperature sensor was modeled to sometimes fail producing an out-of-range value, but other-times fails producing incorrect readings, but not so bad as to be out of range. It is these subtle value errors that occur and propagate in an unrecognized fashion through the system that often cause the most problems.

Much of error analysis is trying to predict the likelihood and effect of undetected errors. How can one model the effect of undetected errors to reliably predict their occurrence and effects in deployed systems? Use EMV2 to explicitly model known unknowns!

The following error state machine models both hard failures (upon hardfail, transition from working to failed), and

```
--error state machine for components that
--may put out undetectable value errors
  error behavior FailSubtle
    use types isolette;
    events
      hardfail: error event;
      subtlefail: error event;
    states
      working: initial state;
      failed : state;
      flakey: state;
    transitions
      working -[hardfail]-> failed;
      working -[subtlefail]-> flakey;
  end behavior;
```

Figure 17: Fail-Subtle Error State Machine

subtle failures (upon softfail, transition from working to flakey).

For components having subcomponents, error models may define their error state in terms of the error states of subcomponents. Figure 18 shows an error machine used when defining composite component behavior.

```
error behavior CompositeFailure
  use types isolette;
  states
    Operational: initial state;
    ReportedFailure: state {DetectedFault};
    MissedFailure: state {MissedAlarm};
    FalseAlarm: state {FalseAlarm};
end behavior;
```

Figure 18: Composite Error State Machine

4.6 Error Flows

AADL includes the notion of *flow* specification that specifies, *e.g.*, that values on a particular input port flow into (are used to calculate the output value) an output. In a similar fashion, error flows specify relationships between input and output ports. However, instead of describing how values are propagated between ports, error flows describe how errors propagate within components. Thus, error flows capture *intra-component* flows. Error propagation between components (*i.e.*, *inter-component* flow) follows architectural connections (*e.g.*, if output port O on component A is connected to input port I on component B, an error may propagate between A and B along this connection). [5]

Error flows may be:

source origin of an error (fault or hazard)

sink detection and/or suppression of incoming error

path transmission of error through component

4.6.1 Error Sources

Error sources model hazard occurrence, deviation in some way from intended behavior.

---

[5]EMV2 has a way to express error flows between components that don't share an explicit connection.

Figure 19 comes from the `temperature_sensor` device stating that `OutOfRange` or `UndetectableValueError` may occur, and will be emitted by the `current_temperature` port.

```
f: error source current_temperature
  {OutOfRange,UndetectableValueError};
```

Figure 19: Error Source

4.6.2 Error Sinks

Error sinks explicitly state that incoming errors are not further propagated.

Any `OutOfRange` error arriving at port `current_temperature` is detected and suppressed.

```
mmmoor: error sink current_temperature
  {OutOfRange};
```

Figure 20: Error Sink

4.6.3 Error Paths

An error path describes how errors flow through components, possibly being transformed into a different type of error.

Either an `ItemOmission` or `ItemComission` error arriving at either port `interface_failure` or `internal_failure` will be transmitted by port `monitor_mode` as a `MonitorModeError`.

A `UndetectableValueError` arriving at port `current_temperature` is also transmitted by port `monitor_mode` as a `MonitorModeError`.

```
mmmiff: error path interface_failure
  {ItemOmission,ItemComission}
      -> monitor_mode(MonitorModeError);
mmminf: error path internal_failure
  {ItemOmission,ItemComission}
      -> monitor_mode(MonitorModeError);
mmmct: error path current_temperature
  {UndetectableValueError}
      -> monitor_mode(MonitorModeError);
```

Figure 21: Error Paths

4.7 Error Detection

Sometimes error models need to cause (or at least influence) behavior, such as when errors are detected by hardware. The Isolette model has a `detect_monitor_failure` device component. Figure 22 shows putting out boolean `internal_failure` signal when in the `failed` state.

4.8 Error Properties

EMV2 annex subclauses may have their own properties. EMV2 properties use core AADL property grammar. The

```
component error behavior
  detections
    failed -[ ]-> internal_failure!;
    --in "failed" state send event out
    --port internal_failure
end component;
```

Figure 22: Error Detection

standard EMV2 property set in EMV2.aadl defines many useful properties for error models.

Figure 23 shows the `detect_monitor_failure` device component type with its EMV2 annex subclause which

- uses types from the standard **ErrorLibrary.aadl**, namely **ItemOmission**

- uses the **FailStop** error state machine shown in Figure 16

- propagates **ItemOmission** from its **internal_failure** port for false-negatives (failing to indicate a problem when it exists)

- does not emit **ItemComission** (false-positives)

- sources the **ItemOmission** errors emitted by its **internal_failure** port, and

- signals **internal_failure** when in failed state

The properties hold the quantitative values of error models.

4.8.1 Occurrence Distribution

The likelihood of errors is defined using EMV2::OccurrenceDistribution properties.

In Figure 23 **fail** is the error event in **FailStop** that triggers transition from **working** to **failed** indicated by port **internal_failure**; and **dmf** is source for **ItemOmission** errors. The occurrence distributions for **fail** and **dmf** are conveniently collected into the **Iso_Properties** property set shown in Figure 24.

Figure 25 shows the beginning of standard, predeclared property set EMV2.aadl. For **Fixed** probability distributions, only the probability value need be specified. The other values of a **DistributionSpecification** are needed by more complex probability distributions.

4.8.2 Occurrence Probability

Error occurrence probability is specified with the **ProbabilityValue** in EMV2::DistributionSpecification. Figure 24 shows the probability values for monitor failure rate, and detection of monitor failure.

4.8.3 Hazards

As indicated above, error sources are hazards. Figure 23 specifies EMV2::Hazard property for error source dmf.ItemOmission.

Figure 26 shows the **Hazard** property defined in EMV2.aadl.

4.8.4 Severity and Likelihood

```
device detect_monitor_failure
features
  internal_failure : out data port
    Base_Types::Boolean
    {BLESS::Assertion =>
      "<<INTERNAL_FAILURE()>>";};
annex EMV2
{**
  use types ErrorLibrary;
  use behavior isolette::FailStop;
error propagations
  internal_failure: out propagation
    {ItemOmission};
  internal_failure: not out propagation
    {ItemComission};
flows
  dmf: error source internal_failure
    {ItemOmission};
end propagations;
component error behavior
  detections
    failed -[ ]-> internal_failure!;
end component;
properties
--failure rate for temp monitor
  EMV2::OccurrenceDistribution =>
    Iso_Properties::MonitorFailureRate
      applies to fail;
--rate of detection failure
  EMV2::OccurrenceDistribution =>
    Iso_Properties::DetectionMonitorFailureRate
      applies to dmf;
--definition of hazard causing failure
  EMV2::Hazard =>
    [ crossreference => "REMH A.5.2.4";
    failure => "monitor failure w/o report";
    phase => "all";
    description => "monitor failure missed";
    comment => "not detecting monitor failures
    loses mitigation of heat control errors";
    ] applies to dmf.ItemOmission;
  ARP4761::Severity => Hazardous
    applies to dmf.ItemOmission;
  ARP4761::Likelihood => ExtremelyImprobable
    applies to dmf.ItemOmission;
**};
end detect_monitor_failure;
```

Figure 23: Detect Monitor Failure Function

```
--rate at which temp monitor fails
  MonitorFailureRate : constant
    EMV2::DistributionSpecification =>
    [ProbabilityValue => 1.6E-7;
    Distribution => Fixed;];
--error rate of detecting monitor failure
  DetectionMonitorFailureRate : constant
    EMV2::DistributionSpecification =>
    [ProbabilityValue => 1.7E-10;
    Distribution => Fixed;];
```

Figure 24: Monitor Failure Rate Properties

EMV2 provides predeclared property sets for both MIL-STD-882 *System Safety Program Requirements/Standard Practice for System Safety* and ARP 4761 *Guidelines and Methods for Conducting Safety Assessment Process on Civil Airborne Systems and Equipment* to declare severity and likeli-

```
property set EMV2
  is
OccurrenceDistribution :
  EMV2::DistributionSpecification
    applies to (all);
DistributionSpecification : type record (
  ProbabilityValue : aadlreal;
  OccurrenceRate : aadlreal;
  MeanValue : aadlreal;
  StandardDeviation : aadlreal;
  ShapeParameter : aadlreal;
  ScaleParameter : aadlreal;
  SuccessCount : aadlreal;
  SampleCount : aadlreal;
  Probability : aadlreal;
  Distribution : EMV2::DistributionFunction;);
DistributionFunction : type enumeration
  (Fixed, Poisson, Exponential,
   Normal, Gauss, Weibull, Binominal);
```

Figure 25: EMV2 Occurrence Distribution Property

```
Hazard: record
  (crossreference: aadlstring;
   failure : aadlstring;
   phase : aadlstring;
   environment : aadlstring;
   description : aadlstring;
   verificationmethod : aadlstring;
   risk : aadlstring;
   comment : aadlstring;) applies to (all);
```

Figure 26: Hazard Property

hood for hazards. Figure 27 shows the property set for ARP 4761 in ARP4791.aadl.

```
property set ARP4761
  is
Severity : inherit enumeration
  (Catastrophic, Hazardous, Major, Minor,
   NoEffect) applies to (all);
Likelihood : inherit enumeration
  (Probable, Remote, ExtremelyRemote,
   ExtremelyImprobable) applies to (all);
end ARP4761;
```

Figure 27: ARP 4761 Severity and Likelihood

In Figure 23, the ARP 4761 severity for failing to report monitor failure was rated Hazardous; its likelihood was rated ExtremelyImprobable.

Certainly, the labels used for ARP 4761 likelihood need to be consistent with probability values. The detection monitor failure rate probability value (Figure 24) is 1.7E-10 which corresponds to ExtremelyImprobable: $p < 10^{-9}$.

Whereas likelihood has mathematical specificity, severity is inherently subjective and discontinuous. ARP 4761 defines severity levels Catastrophic, Hazardous, Major, Minor, NoEffect.

The notion of Risk Priority Number (RPN) as currently practiced in Failure Modes, Effects, and *Criticality* Analysis gives failure severity a number, and then multiplies by failure likelihood (then divides by "likelihood of detection") to determine risk priority. This notion has a major, even unacceptable, limitation. It models a continuous function that can bury, or hide, more severe categories by less severe categories. For instance, a Catastrophic error that results in death (criticality = 5) might be quite infrequent and highly detectable so that its RPN is a lower value than a more frequent, less detectable Hazardous or Major error that results in injury or pain (criticality = 3 or 4); this situation, which is not unusual, would obscure the Catastrophic error that results in death. Severity, or criticality, for medical devices is not continuous, it has step changes between categories. Each error within Catastrophic or Hazardous categories should be examined with its own separate FMEA.

Consequently, RPN and quantifying severity commits category error; some things cannot be measured by a single number: Instead, risk analysis must treat each class of severity distinctly, with greatest interest in errors that can kill. Proper classification of hazards is thus supremely important and should be performed by the most senior and experienced system engineers in conjunction with domain experts.

5. EMV2 ANALYSIS TOOLS

The EMV2 plug-in to OSATE comes with several analysis tools. They analyze and process EMV2 descriptions attached to an AADL architecture for evaluating system safety or reliability. They produce either document or evidence of software faults or defects.

The following section gives an overview of the toolset and its capabilities but does not provide guidance for using the tools. Users that are looking for help and support may refer to OSATE help [17] or the SEI technical report about the specific Error-Model Toolset [2],

5.1 Instance vs Declarative Models

Although people write text expressing declarative models, all EMV2 analysis tools process instance models. Understanding the difference is crucial to using these EMV2 tools. Instance models are generated from declarative models by OSATE. For very simple systems, declarative and instance models can be practically identical when there is only one design choice. The distinction between declarative and instance models can be hard to grasp, but once understood seems obvious.

Declarative models can include many design options. In the textual, declarative model, components may have several levels of subtyping; particular component types may have more than one implementation; components may use AADL's prototypes to describe a class of designs using parametric polymorphism; component implementations may have arrays of subcomponents; component features may be arrays of ports.

Instance models are built from declarative models and represent a particular design, out of possibly many. To generate an instance model from a declarative model, a component implementation is selected. The instantiation function then resolves all the polymorphisms into concrete types, and creates a data structure for each component in the system. If component arrays are used, a data structure for each element is created.

Figure 28 shows a graphical view of the architecture instance of the Isolette model defined in Figure 29. It shows the system components (temperature_sensor, operator_inter-

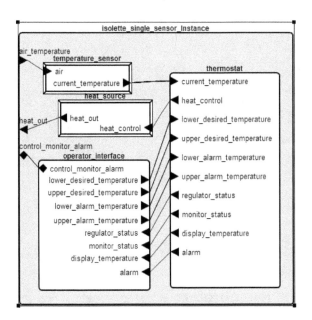

Figure 28: Instance Model of the Isolette Model

face, `heat_source`, `thermostat`) and their interconnection. Such representation is provided by the Instance Model Viewer (IMV) within OSATE [17].

5.2 Graphical View of Error Impacts

The Instance Model Viewer (IMV) of OSATE provides graphical support for representing AADL instance models with their associated error annotations. When selecting a component, the tool highlights its impacts when failing. Depending on the connection level between components, the color brightness changes (a dark color means that the component is more likely to be impacted by the selected component). An example of this function is shown in figure 30: components in dark red (`operator_interface` and `heat_-source`) are impacted by any fault occurring within the `temperature_sensor`. While it does not distinguish the different error types within the architecture, this function provides an overview of the impact of a failure of a component.

5.3 Consistency Checks

The OSATE toolset provides a function to check the consistency of the error declaration against other architecture artifacts. For example, below are some of the rules that are enforced by the consistency check:

- an `error sink` cannot be used as a `propagation condition` for propagating other errors through the component features.

- switching from one `error state` to another can be triggered only when receiving an error on an `error sink`.

- in an `error transition`, all `error events` and incoming error propagations must be referenced

- two `component error behavior` transitions cannot have the same condition

All consistency checks are listed in [2] related to the Error-Model Annex and its OSATE support [17].

```
system implementation isolette.single_sensor
subcomponents
  thermostat : system
    thermostat_single_sensor.impl;
  temperature_sensor : device
    Devices::temperature_sensor.impl;
  heat_source : device
    Devices::heat_source.impl;
  operator_interface : system
    operator_interface.impl;
connections
  ct : port
    temperature_sensor.current_temperature
    -> thermostat.current_temperature;
  hc : port thermostat.heat_control
    -> heat_source.heat_control;
  ldt : port
    operator_interface.lower_desired_temperature
    -> thermostat.lower_desired_temperature;
  udt : port
    operator_interface.upper_desired_temperature
    -> thermostat.upper_desired_temperature;
  lat : port
    operator_interface.lower_alarm_temperature
    -> thermostat.lower_alarm_temperature;
  uat : port
    operator_interface.upper_alarm_temperature
    -> thermostat.upper_alarm_temperature;
  rs : port thermostat.regulator_status
    -> operator_interface.regulator_status;
  ms : port thermostat.monitor_status
    -> operator_interface.monitor_status;
  dt : port thermostat.display_temperature
    -> operator_interface.display_temperature;
  al : port thermostat.alarm
    -> operator_interface.alarm;
annex EMV2
  {**
  use types ErrorLibrary, Isolette;
  use behavior CompositeFailure;
  composite error behavior
  states
  [temperature_sensor.failed
    or thermostat.ReportedFailure
    or heat_source.failed]->ReportedFailure;
  [temperature_sensor.flakey
    or thermostat.MissedFailure]->MissedFailure;
  end composite;
  **};
end isolette.single_sensor;
```

Figure 29: Declarative Text Model of Single-Sensor Isolette

This function also looks at all connections and checks for incoming/outgoing specification consistency. If any error types from the `out` propagation are not included in the error types expected by the incoming propagation, the tool reports an error. This function highlight potential defects and helps one understand if the architecture handles all potential faults. This is of particular interest when integrating components from different models and development teams.

For example, considering that a component is an `error source` for error types `UndetectableValueError` and `ItemOmission` errors, changing the receiver specification from

```
display_temperature: in propagation
  {UndetectableValueError,ItemOmission};
```

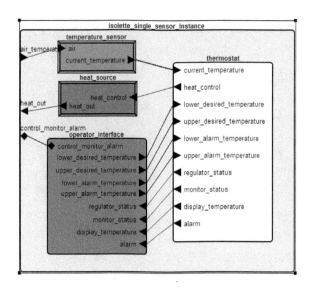

Figure 30: Highlight errors in the Instance Model

to

```
display_temperature: in propagation
   {UndetectableValueError};
```

will trigger an consistency error because the `ItemOmission` type is no longer handled by the receiver.

The toolset will then report an error such as: *"Outgoing propagation displayed_temp { UndetectableValueError, ItemOmission} has error types not handled by incoming propagation display_temperature { UndetectableValueError}"*.

5.4 Fault Hazard Assessment

A conventional Functional Hazard Assessment (FHA) is an exhaustive enumeration of all failure conditions in the architecture. It lists all error contributors and reports their associated information (likelihood, description, severity, etc.). Such a document identifies all potential sources of errors and is required by safety validation standard such as ARP4761 [16].

OSATE supports the production of FHA reports. To do so, it analyzes the architecture, extracts all potential error contributors (**error source**, **error event**) and their associated documentation (EMV2 properties such as `EMV2::Hazards`, `EMV2::Severity` and `EMV2::Likelihood`) and generated a spreadsheet that aggregates all this information. A complete description of this function is described in [2]. Figure 31 shows an excerpt of the Isolette Fault and Hazard Assessment report. For each component, it lists the error sources and their associated information (error, cross-reference to other documents, effect, etc.).

5.5 Fault-Tree Analysis

A conventional Fault-Tree Analysis (FTA) is a graphical representation of the contributor to a failure state. This is a top-down approach, showing the resulting error state at the top and listing all its contributors within the architecture. It makes use of the tree notation to show the dependency between error events. Such analysis is especially valuable when analyzing a system and inspecting all components that

may contribute to a system failure. Such a technique is required by safety evaluation process such as ARP4761 [16].

OSATE supports the automatic generation of FTAs, constructed by analyzing the architecture and error propagation paths. Figure 32 presents an example of an FTA for the Isolette. The top-level element represents the error state under investigation while the other nodes represent contributing error states/events. OSATE supports the generation of FTA for both open-source (such as OpenFTA [15]) and commercial tools (such as CAFTA).

5.6 Fault Impact

OSATE provides a Fault Impact Analysis that automatically traces the error paths from error sources to affected components. Contrary to the Fault-Tree Analysis, this is a bottom-up approach that lists all impacted components for each error source. While the resulting report document can be quite long, it may be useful when considering faults of a particular component and documenting their impact on the overall architecture. Such a document is similar to FMEA (Failure Mode and Effects Analysis) or FMES (Failure Modes and Effects Summary) required by safety-validation standards, such as ARP4761 [16].

Table 1 shows an extract of the Fault Impact document generated from the Isolette AADL model, depicting the fault impact of `OutOfRange` errors from the `temperature` sensor. The first (non-header) indicates that when the temperature sensor has failed such that its current temperature value is out of range, that error will be received by the `manage_monitor_mode` thread in the `monitor_temperature` process, where it will be detected and masked. The document then contains the list of all error sources and their propagations across the overall architecture.

5.7 Reliability Block Diagram

A Reliability Block Diagram (RBD) provides the reliability value for a using the system components and their relationships. Each component is treated as an isolated block that has a designated reliability or failure rate value. The computation of the reliability measure depends on the na-

	A	B	C	D	E	F	G
1	Component	Error	Crossreference	Functional Failure (Hazard)	Environment	Effects of Hazard	Comment
2	temperature_sensor	"hardfail"	"REMH A.3.2"	"total failure"	"infant intensive care"	"temperature sensor breaks"	"easily detected and alarm issued"
3	temperature_sensor	"subtlefail"	"REMH A.3.2"	"bad value"	"infant intensive care"	"temperature sensor out of calibration"	"undetectable"
4	heat_source	"fail"	"REMH A.3.2"	"heat source breaks"	"infant intensive care"	"mechanical disconnection of heat source"	"always fails open (off)"

Figure 31: Example of the Fault Hazard Assessment for the Isolette Model

Table 1: Single-Sensor Out-of-Range Fault Impact Analysis

Component	Initial Failure Mode	1st Level Effect	Failure Mode
temperature_sensor	failed	current_temperature {OutOfRange} -> monitor_temperature/ manage_monitor_mode	monitor_temperature/ manage_monitor_mode.current_temperature {OutOfRange} [Masked]
temperature_sensor	failed	current_temperature {OutOfRange} -> regulate_temperature/ manage_regulator_interface	regulate_temperature/ manage_regulator_interface.current_temperature {OutOfRange} [Masked]
temperature_sensor	failed	current_temperature {OutOfRange} -> regulate_temperature/ manage_heat_source	regulate_temperature/ manage_heat_source.current_temperature {OutOfRange} [Masked]
temperature_sensor	failed	current_temperature {OutOfRange} -> regulate_temperature/ manage_regulator_mode	regulate_temperature/ manage_regulator_mode.current_temperature {OutOfRange} [Masked]

ture of component interactions (connection in series, parallel, etc.). A complete description of the algorithm is presented in [2]). Such a notation is used by several safety evaluation standards, such as ARP4761, which refer to this representation as a Dependency Diagram (DD).

OSATE supports the generation of a reliability report by computing the reliability value for an error state. The tool does not generate the graphical notation of the RDB but provides the reliability value using failure probability of AADL components. A complete description of this feature is detailed in [2].

5.8 Markov Chain Analysis

A Markov model (a.k.a. chain) represents a system behavior with its states and transitions. It also assigns a probability to each transition. Then, dedicated tools can process this notation, simulate the system behavior or analyze it to evaluate the probability for being in a particular state. Such analysis is required by safety evaluation standards such as ARP4761 [16] and is especially useful to validate a component reliability (probability that a component fails is less than a fixed given value).

OSATE transforms AADL error models into Markov models so that safety engineers use the architecture notation to evaluate its safety. For now, produced Markov models can be used with PRISM [10], an open-source tool for analyzing Markov Chain model. A complete description of that function is included in [2].

6. CONCLUSION AND FUTURE WORK

We believe that risk assessments and safety analyses too often end up being inconsistent and tedious to perform, and that opportunities are missed to reuse and leverage information across different techniques. Moreover, overall accuracy

and the ability to to establish rigorous traceability to is hindered by the fact that techniques are not directly integrated artifacts directly tied to implementations.

Modeling in AADL and EMV2 provides engineers of high-integrity systems with techniques and tools that can enable a more rigorous, automated, and integrated approach to important risk management activities. The formalization by EMV2 of error models enables better support for automation of hazard analysis techniques, and ensures that all such analyses apply to the same, single-source of truth. The integration with formal architectural descriptions written in AADL enables strong traceability to artifacts directly tied to implementations (especially in situations where implementation source code for system interfaces is automatically generated from a system's AADL-based architectural specification). When we have presented this approach to software developers, many have indicated that similarities and analogies to code-level annotation-based tools, static analysis, and type checking make the AADL EMV2-based approach much more attractive than conventional approaches.

In this paper, we have illustrated basic aspects of EMV2 on a simple medical device and drawn connections to standard techniques such as FMEA and FTA. Two major directions for future work include (a) applying EMV2 to systems of greater scale and complexity, and (b) illustrating how AADL EMV2 supports other safety/risk-related analyses. Regarding (a), engineers at SEI are applying EMV2 to more complex avionics systems, and illustrating the use of EMV2 in large-scale avionics integration is an emphasis in ongoing work on the SAVI project. In our own research group and in collaborations with FDA engineers, we are applying EMV2 to AADL models of a realistic infusion pump [11]. We are also laying the groundwork for application of AADL and EMV2 to specifying the ASTM 2761 standard

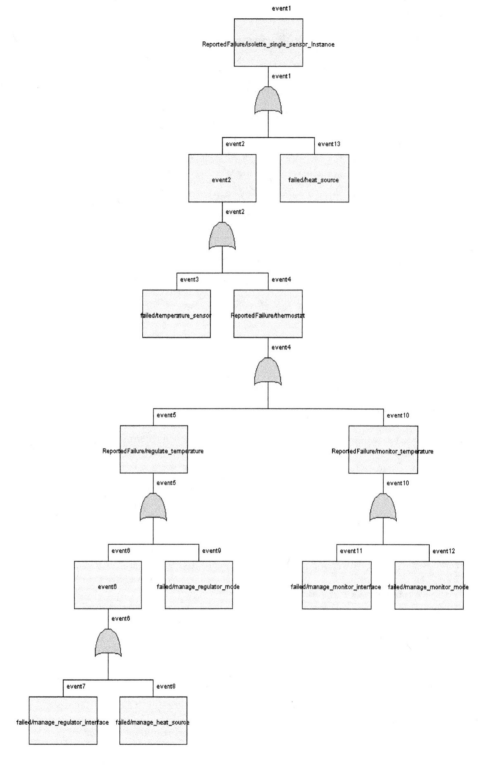

Figure 32: Example of the Fault-Tree for the Isolette Model

Integrated Clinical Environment (ICE) architecture to support development, safety certification, and FDA regulatory review of medical application platforms [9]. These later activities are also supporting efforts on the UL/AAMI Joint Committee on Medical Device Interoperability to develop safety standards for systems of interoperable medical devices.

Regarding (b), since AADL and EMV2 are being used on avionics projects such as SAVI, it seems worthwhile to expand the discussion on how EMV2 supports various safety-related analyses to include a broader of overview of how the methodology and techniques in ARP 4761 could be supported.

Acknowledgements

This work is supported in part by the US National Science Foundation (NSF) (#0932289, #1239543), the NSF US Food and Drug Administration Scholar-in-Residence Program (#1065887, #1238431) the National Institutes of Health / NIBIB Quantum Program, and the US Air Force Office of Scientific Research (AFOSR) (#FA9550-09-1-0138). The authors wish to thank Peter Feiler from SEI and engineers from the US Food and Drug Administration for feedback on this work. Peter Feiler is the author of the EMV2 annex, and his work provides the foundation for the example-based presentation of this paper.

7. REFERENCES

[1] Architecture Analysis & Design Language. www.aadl.info, 2012.

[2] J. Delange, P. Feiler, D. Gluch, and J. Hudak. AADL fault modeling and analysis within an ARP4761 safety assessment. Technical report, Carnegie Mellon Software Engineering Institute, 2013.

[3] E. S. Dominique Blouin, Skander Turki. AADL requirements annex (draft, progress update). |https://wiki.sei.cmu.edu/aadl/images/a/af/Requirements_annex_aadl_standards_meeting_16-19_04_2012.pdf|.

[4] C. A. Ericson. *Hazard Analysis Techniques for System Safety*. Wiley-Interscience, 2005.

[5] P. Feiler. *Architecture Analysis and Design Language (AADL) Annex Volume 3: Annex E: Error Model V2 Annex*. Number SAE AS5506/3 (Draft) in SAE Aerospace Standard. SAE International, 2013.

[6] P. Feiler and D. Gluch. *Model-Based Engineering with AADL: An Introduction to the SAE Architecture Analysis and Design Language*. Addison-Wesley, 2012.

[7] P. H. Feiler, J. Hansson, D. de Niz, and L. Wrage. System architecture virtual integration: An industrial case study. Technical Report CMU/SEI-2009-TR-017, CMU, 2009.

[8] P. Fenelon and J. A. Mcdermid. An integrated toolset for software safety analysis. *Journal of Systems and Software*, 21:279–290, 1993.

[9] J. Hatcliff, A. King, I. Lee, A. Fernandez, A. McDonald, E. Vasserman, and S. Weininger. Rationale and architecture principles for medical application platforms. In *Proceedings of the 2012 International Conference on Cyberphysical Systems*, 2012.

[10] M. Kwiatkowska, G. Norman, and D. Parker. PRISM 4.0: Verification of probabilistic real-time systems. In G. Gopalakrishnan and S. Qadeer, editors, *Proc. 23rd International Conference on Computer Aided Verification (CAV'11)*, volume 6806 of *LNCS*, pages 585–591. Springer, 2011.

[11] B. R. Larson, J. Hatcliff, and P. Chalin. Open source patient-controlled analgesic pump requirements documentation. In *Proceedings of the International Workshop on Software Engineering in Healthcare*, San Francisco, May 2013.

[12] D. Lempia and S. Miller. DOT/FAA/AR-08/32. Requirements Engineering Management Handbook, 2009.

[13] N. Leveson. *Safeware: System Safety and Computers*. Addison-Wesley, 1995.

[14] N. Leveson. *Engineering a Safer World: Systems Thinking Applied to Safety*. MIT Press, 2012.

[15] O-Sys. OpenFTA - http://www.openfta.com, 2013.

[16] SAE International. *ARP4761 - Guidelines and Methods for Conducting the Safety Assessment Process on Civil Airborne Systems and Equipment*, 1996.

[17] SEI/CMU. Open Source AADL Tool Environment (OSATE) - `https://wiki.sei.cmu.edu/aadl`, 2013.

[18] M. Wallace. Modular architectural representation and analysis of fault propagation and transformation. In *Proc. FESCA 2005, ENTCS 141(3), Elsevier*, pages 53–71, 2005.

[19] System Architecture Virtual Integration (SAVI) Initiative. `https://wiki.sei.cmu.edu/aadl/index.php/Projects_and_Initiatives#AVSI_SAVI`wiki.sei.cmu.edu/aadl/index.php/Projects_and_Initiatives, 2012.

Formal Methods: An Industrial Perspective

Jeannette M. Wing
Microsoft Research
One Microsoft Way
Redmond, WA 98052
+1 425-706-4459
wing@microsoft.com

ABSTRACT

Formal methods research has made tremendous progress since the 1980s when a proof using a theorem prover was worthy of a Ph.D. thesis and a bug in a VLSI textbook was found using a model checker. Now, with advances in theorem proving, model checking, satisfiability modulo theories (SMT) solvers, and program analysis, the engines of formal methods are more sophisticated and are applicable and scalable: to a wide range of domains, from biology to mathematics; to a wide range of systems, from asynchronous systems to spreadsheets; and for a wide range of properties, from security to program termination. In this talk, I will present a few Microsoft Research stories of advances in formal methods and their application to Microsoft products and services. Formal methods use, however, is not routine—yet—in industrial practice. So, I will close with outstanding challenges and new directions for research in formal methods.

Categories and Subject Descriptors

D.2 [**Software Engineering**], D.2.4 [**Software/Program Verification**]

General Terms

Reliability, Languages, Verification.

Keywords

Formal methods, specification, verification, theorem proving, model checking, satisfiability modulo theories, constraint satisfaction, program synthesis

HILT'13, November 10–14, 2013, Pittsburgh, PA, USA.
ACM 978-1-4503-2467-0/13/11.
http://dx.doi.org/10.1145/2527269.2527291

Automatic versus Interactive Program Verification

Suad Alagić
Department of Computer Science
University of Southern Maine
alagic@usm.maine.edu

ABSTRACT

We report on experiences in using two very different program verification technologies. One of them is based on object-oriented assertion languages and it comes with automatic static verification of object-oriented programs. The other technology is independent of a programming language or programming paradigm and it offers static interactive verification of very complex constraints. These two technologies were applied to the problem of static verification of object-oriented transactions. The problem was chosen because database technologies are not equipped to handle general integrity constraints and verification technologies are not used to verify transactions. The implications of static verification on data integrity, efficiency, and reliability of transactions are significant.

Categories and Subject Descriptors

D.2.4 [**Software**]: Program Verification, Assertion checkers; F.3.1 [**Specifying and Verifying and Reasoning about Programs**]: Assertions, Mechanical verification ; H.2.4 [**Systems**]: Object-oriented databases, Transaction processing

General Terms

Verification

Keywords

Constraints; Verification; Transactions

1. TRANSACTION VERIFICATION

The current object technology has nontrivial problems in specifying and enforcing even classical database integrity constraints, let alone more general integrity constraints. More general constraints come from complex application environments and they are often critical for correct functioning of those applications. Such constraints cannot be expressed in a declarative fashion in mainstream object-oriented programming languages because those languages by themselves have no such capabilities.

Since the integrity constraints cannot be specified in a declarative fashion, the only option is to enforce them procedurally with nontrivial implications on efficiency and reliability. This is why database systems support very limited integrity constraints, such as keys and referential integrity. Expensive recovery procedures may be required when a transaction violates the constraints at run-time.

Our approach is based on the usage of object-oriented assertion and logic-based languages and verification systems for expressing and enforcing very general integrity constraints. The main goal is to statically verify that transactions maintain the constraints in order to avoid nontrivial problems when the constraints are violated at run-time.

The idea of static verification of transaction safety with respect to the database integrity constraints was first published in [6]. More recent results are [2, 3, 1]. In our technology an object-oriented schema is a class equipped with a variety of constraints, including the classical database constraints such as keys and referential integrity. There is general bounded parametric transaction class. A specific transaction is defined with respect to a specific schema by instantiating the generic transaction class with that schema. The actual transaction action is specified with a precondition and a postcondition.

Transaction verification amounts to verifying the following: If the schema invariant and the transaction precondition hold at the transaction start, the schema invariant and the transaction postcondition will hold at the transaction commit point. A related problem is verifying that if a transaction is started, it will eventually either commit of abort. And finally, after transaction abort the schema invariant should also hold, i.e., a consistent database state must be restored.

In our technology, a transaction that fails static verification will never be executed. Knowing in advance that a transaction will violate the integrity constraints makes a nontrivial difference in most complex application environments. Not allowing execution of such a transaction eliminates the consequences of running such a transaction against the database: violation of data integrity and invocation of recovery procedures.

2. AUTOMATIC STATIC VERIFICATION

Automatic static verification is in our work based on Spec# [4]. Spec# is an object-oriented assertion language for C#.

HILT'13, November 10–14, 2013, Pittsburgh, PA, USA.
ACM 978-1-4503-2467-0/13/11.
http://dx.doi.org/10.1145/2527269.2527281 ...$15.00.

It extends C# with quite general constraints and has a verifying compiler that checks whether the C# code satisfies the assertions. Spec# extends the C# type system with non-null object types. It also has a sophisticated ownership model which mainstream object-oriented languages do not have.

3. INTERACTIVE STATIC VERIFICATION

Interactive static verification is in our work represented by the PVS technology (Prototype Verification System) [5]. PVS is a general tool not tied to any specific programming language. It has a type system with features of type systems of modern programming languages such as genericity (parametric polymorphism). PVS allows specification of much more general constraints than those expressible in assertion languages. PVS is a higher-order system which means that it allows definition of specialized logics that are suitable for particular applications.

4. STATIC VERSUS DYNAMIC VERIFICATION

While our goal is to statically eliminate transactions that provably violate the schema integrity constraints or their own specification in terms of pre and post conditions, the fact that transactions operate on persistent objects has several nontrivial implications. One of them is that some dynamic checks are still necessary. This is why dynamic checks that Spec# generates are important. Such checks are hard to generate with PVS. They require decision procedures and invocation of the prover at run-time. Although that has been done, we find it impractical and have not experimented with it.

The problems of static versus dynamic transaction verification is the following. Static verification applies to the transaction code. But if a transaction is invoked with arguments that do not satisfy the precondition or the schema invariant does not hold, the verification results do not apply. This is why dynamic checks are essential.

The transaction should handle the exceptions caused by dynamic checks properly. Static verification guarantees that in the absence of such exceptions or if they are correctly handled, the results of transaction execution will be correct with respect to the integrity constraints. But if a transaction fails static verification, it will not compile, and hence it will not be executed.

A typical case of a dynamic check is verifying that the transaction precondition holds at the transaction start point. For example, inserting a new object into a collection of objects equipped with the key constraint requires a dynamic check that the key of the newly inserted object does not already exist in the collection. But then static verification will guarantee that the postcondition will hold, and it does not have to be dynamically checked.

5. CONCLUSIONS

The verification techniques presented in the paper allow largely static verification of transactions with respect to the data integrity constraints. The integrity constraints could be very general, at least as general as those expressible in object-oriented assertion languages. The implications on data integrity, efficiency and reliability of transactions are obvious and non-trivial.

Data integrity and runtime reliability of transactions are significantly improved. Expensive recovery procedures may often be avoided. In addition, more general application constraints that are not necessarily database constraints could be specified and enforced. We are not aware of any other transaction technology with these properties.

Automatic static verification (as in Spec#) is clearly a preferable verification technology from the viewpoint of the users. At this point that technology is still a prototype. The underlying architecture that separates the view of the users from the prover technology is very complex. Static verification sometimes comes with difficulties.

Interactive verification as represented by PVS allows reasoning about constraints that are not expressible in the assertion languages, and verification techniques that complement the support that the assertion languages have in terms of static and dynamic enforcement of constraints. However, this technology requires very sophisticated users with mathematical background that typical programmers do not have. Proofs are not easy to manage and development of proof strategies for particular problem areas is required.

The final conclusion is that future research should attempt to develop sophisticated programming environments in which automatic and interactive verification techniques are offered within a user-oriented unified framework.

Another general conclusion follows from our experiences in solving the transaction verification problem. Static verification is obviously a preferable strategy. However, there are application areas in which static verification is not enough. At least some dynamic tests of constraints are still required, as the problem of transaction verification demonstrates.

Acknowledgement

This paper is a summary of our experiences in static transaction verification. My students that participated in this work are Adnan Fazeli, Ben Chandler, Ruchi Jareith and Harika Anumula. Specific results and the mathematical theory are the topics of separate papers.

6. REFERENCES

[1] S. Alagić and A. Fazeli, Verifiable object-oriented transactions, Proceedings of COB 2012 (Concurrent Objects and Beyond), *LNCS*, to appear.

[2] S. Alagić, P. Bernstein, and R. Jairath, Object-oriented constraints for XML Schema, Proceedings of ICOODB 2010, *LNCS 6348*, pp. 101-118.

[3] I. G. Baltopoulos, J. Borgstrom, and A. G. Gordon, Maintaining database integrity with refinement types, Proceedings of ECOOP 2011, *LNCS 6813*, pp. 484-509, 2011.

[4] Microsoft Corp., Spec#, http://research.microsoft.com/specsharp/.

[5] S. Owre, N. Shankar, J. M. Rushby, and D. W. J. Stringer-Clavert: PVS Language Reference, SRI International, Computer Science Laboratory, http://pvs.csl.sri.com/doc/pvs-language-reference.pdf.

[6] T. Sheard and D. Stemple, Automatic verification of database transaction safety, *ACM TODS 14*, pp. 322-368, 1989.

Author Index

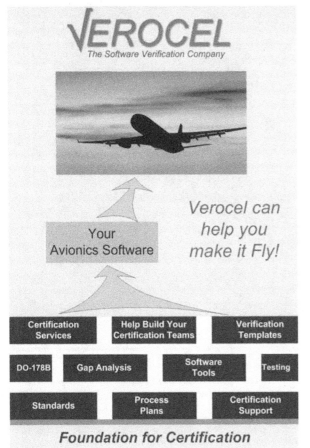

www.ingramcontent.com/pod-product-compliance
Lightning Source LLC
LaVergne TN
LVHW060146070326
832902LV00018B/2976